In *Embracing Your Life Sentence* Lonnell Johnson offers a practical guidebook written in response to prostate cancer. You'll enjoy how he masterfully weaves original poetry with scripture in this inspirational book. His message of hope can be applied to overcome any adversity.

—Kary Oberbrunner, author of Elixir Project, Your Secret Name, and The Deeper Path

Lonnell Johnson, Ph.D., is a man of faith, a man with cancer yet surviving and a patient in my practice for many years. He has decided in his cancer journey to take the road less traveled and is not only yet holding on but is flourishing in spite of the difficulties encountered. His testimony is a tale worth telling and sharing. I encourage all to read his fascinating journey's story, one whose final chapter is not yet written.

—Rueben N. Rivers, MD

Embracing Your Life Sentence: How to Turn Life's Greatest Tragedies into Your Greatest Triumphs

Lonnell E. Johnson, Ph.D.

Copyright © 2018

By Lonnell E. Johnson, Ph.D.

First Edition

All rights reserved

No portion of this book may be reproduced, stored in a retrieval system, or transmitted in any form or by any means without written permission of the publisher.

Paperback: 978-1-64085-403-1

Hardback: 978-1-64085-404-8

Ebook: 978-1-64085-405-5

Disclaimer: The content of *Embracing Your Life Sentence: How to Turn Life's Greatest Tragedies into Your Greatest Triumphs* is based on the personal experiences of the author, Lonnell E. Johnson, prostate cancer survivor. The information is presented for educational purposes only and is not intended to diagnose nor prescribe for any medical or psychological condition, nor to prevent, treat, mitigate or cure such conditions. The information contained herein is not intended to replace a one-on-one relationship with a doctor or qualified healthcare professional. This information, therefore, is not intended as medical advice, but rather a sharing of knowledge and information based on personal research and experience. Lonnell E. Johnson encourages readers to make their own health care decisions based on their judgment and research in partnership with a qualified healthcare professional.

CONTENTS

Introduction 1

Chapter 1   "You've Got Cancer"—
Responding to the Diagnosis. 3

Chapter 2   Watchman: Watch Your Mouth and
Other Matters. 8

Chapter 3   Fighter: The fight of my life,
the fight for my life. 17

Chapter 4   Prayer Warrior: Demonstrating
the Power of Prayer 36

Chapter 5   The Fear Factor: "Do not fear;
I will help you" 48

Chapter 6   The Faith Factor:
Without Faith it is Impossible. 54

Chapter 7   The Forgiveness Factor:
A Forgotten Component. 67

Chapter 8   A Setback: Perfecting the Art of Patience. 84

Chapter 9   Embracing Your Life Sentence—
My Strategy in Summary. 101

Acknowledgements 115

About the Author 119

INTRODUCTION

"You've got cancer:" spoken to me in 2000, these three words changed my life forever. After taking time to process the diagnosis of prostate cancer, I did not see it as a death sentence, but I came to see it as a life sentence that transformed my thinking. *Embracing Your Life Sentence: How to Turn Life's Greatest Tragedies into Your Greatest Triumphs* is that life-changing process. I will share with you some of the keys and principles applied in developing a holistic strategy in response to a cancer diagnosis. In the process, I discovered a divine invitation with greater possibilities and recognized that the trials we currently face are part of a much larger story. As I journeyed down the road less traveled, I learned to watch, fight and pray; I emerged not only a survivor but more than a conqueror over cancer or any other adversity I might face.

More than 50 years ago after being drafted into the Army during the Viet Nam era, I experienced a powerful conversion that introduced me to the transforming power of God through receiving the Holy Spirit and studying of the Bible. Since then, my approach to any adverse situation has been to go to the Scriptures to seek guidance and direction in applying the principles I find. In relating my findings, I point to specific passages, citing chapter and verse as I comment, as I do in this book.

Although I published *Watch, Fight & Pray: My Personal Three-Fold Strategy to Overcome Prostate Cancer* in 2005, the booklet is no longer in print, but it laid the foundation for *Embracing Your Life Sentence: How to Turn Life's Greatest Tragedies into Your Greatest Triumphs* which explores in far greater detail aspects of the body, soul, and spirit which impacted my response to the diagnosis. In addition, chapters are devoted to principles applied as a watchman, fighter, and prayer warrior in the battle against prostate cancer. *Embracing Your Life Sentence* also examines three other factors influencing my diagnosis: fear, forgiveness, and faith. A chapter is devoted to each of these factors, using scriptural references along with personal experiences with practical application, and other sources focusing on spiritual components that contribute to the healing process. I also share my experiences as a former hospital pharmacist who prepared chemotherapy for in-patients at the time. In addition, as a practicing poet, I include original poetry and song lyrics along with commentary which add a distinctive flavor to this book which has been a challenging labor of love to produce.

1

"YOU'VE GOT CANCER"— RESPONDING TO THE DIAGNOSIS

Never deny a diagnosis, but do deny the negative verdict that may go with it.

—Norman Cousins

"You've got cancer." Three simple words echoed through my mind as I responded to the statement with a question—"What?" It wasn't that I didn't hear the statement, but I asked in disbelief. Each time I raised the question I gave the same response, similar to the repeated voice mail announcement *you've got mail* reverberating in my head, only with a more sobering consequence. Receiving a diagnosis of cancer alters your perspective of life forever. I know those three words profoundly impacted my life.

In 2000 after my annual physical examination revealed my prostate-specific antigen (PSA)—a blood factor used to assess the state of the prostate gland—had increased, my physician recommended I see a urologist. After consultation, he took a biopsy of the prostate which revealed that I had a small amount of cancer in the core of the gland.

While the words *you've got cancer* resounded in my ears, the urologist mentioned three possible treatment options: surgery, radiation, or chemotherapy. Without hesitation, he went on to ask, "When do you want to schedule the surgery?" I paused, took a deep breath, and said, "I need time to process what you just said and to pray and ask God what I should do." After what seemed like several minutes of absolute silence, I said, "I'll get back with you later and let you know my decision."

As a former hospital pharmacist who compounded and often dispensed chemotherapy, I immediately knew I did not want to go that route. Because of the potentially life-changing consequences of surgery and radiation, these two options were also not acceptable. Impotence and incontinence were all too real possible side-effects. Having to wear adult diapers as a way of life was also disturbing to think about.

After leaving the urologist's office, I went home and informed my wife, Brenda, of the doctor's announcement, his advice, and my determination to trust God to be healed. I also met with my pastor at the time, Eric Warren, my trusted friend and brother-in-law, and we prayed together. We both touched and agreed that God would intervene in the situation so that I would be healed. As we departed, I chuckled and said, "Maybe Christ will return, and I won't have to worry about it, after all." This was another real possibility to consider, as I pondered what I would say to the urologist.

Quite providentially at the time of my diagnosis, our church was observing a period called Seven Days of Stillness, an exercise designed to bring Christian believers into a closer relationship with God through prayer, specific readings from the Bible, and other activities. I observed the Seven Days of Stillness, as I sought the Lord regarding a strategy to address the situation with my increasing PSA count and cancer diagnosis. During this time, God assured me that I was not to panic nor become alarmed and do something rash. "Be still and know that I am God," so the Psalmist declares, and I followed suit with a confident heart at peace with God who has expressed His love to me in so many ways so many times before.

Later when I met with the urologist, I gathered as much information as I could on prostate cancer and treatment options, mainly alternative possibilities. After much prayerful consideration, I chose to adopt a posture of watchful waiting or active surveillance, monitoring my PSA with doctor's visits every six months instead of yearly. Although prostate cancer is slow growing initially, it can become more aggressive in later stages and can metastasize to the bone or other organs, so it is essential to monitor these possibilities. In addition to these measures, I made changes in diet and nutrition, along with other naturopathic remedies, including herbs, and detoxing my body with deep internal cleansing.

I continued this monitoring procedure for ten years, and in 2011, I participated in a clinical trial for the treatment of prostate cancer involving bread made from a soy and almond combination at the James Cancer Center at Ohio State University. Since relocating to North Carolina in 2013, I have continued my vigil of watching and waiting.

"You've Got Cancer."—Closing Comments.

A cancer diagnosis itself can unleash a stream of negative emotions in some individuals: fear, anger, along with a numbing sense of disbelief; in others, a defiant denial erupts. Some well-meaning Christians, when given a diagnosis of cancer, will emphatically respond with "I don't received that!" Some whom I knew would not even acknowledge the diagnosis and defiantly proclaimed they did *not* have cancer. Unfortunately, within varying lengths of time, they died as a result of the disease they insisted they did not have.

EMBRACING YOUR LIFE SENTENCE

While investigating possible treatment for prostate cancer, I came across a statement from Norman Cousins, who offered this sound advice to cancer patients:

> Never deny a diagnosis, but do deny the negative verdict that may go with it.

Over the years, I have learned some people, however, relate a cancer diagnosis with a death sentence. Cancer does not always equate to death due to cancer. Diagnoses are facts based on tests or information gathered and analyzed at a particular time. Facts can change, and so can a diagnosis.

After my diagnosis, I inquired of the Lord as to what I should do. Out of an intense period of reflection and prayer came the inspiration for my personal three-fold strategy. I share what it means to watch, related to the body, the physical aspects of this devastating disease. Secondly, I also learned to fight the good fight of faith and come to grips with the mental or emotional components of the soul. Finally, I learned to recognize the spiritual components of the diagnosis, such as faith, forgiveness, and most importantly, the power of prayer. All of this I share in the unfolding chapters of *Embracing Your Life Sentence: How to Turn Life's Greatest Tragedies into Your Greatest Triumphs*.

Each chapter closes with an original poem, a psalm written to capture the essence of that particular message:

Watching, Waiting, Seeking

*"Wait on the LORD; be of good courage,
and He shall strengthen your heart;
wait, I say, on the LORD!"*
—Psalm 27:14

"YOU'VE GOT CANCER"

Reassured once more we will not be left behind,
But with patience we must still learn to watch and wait.
We look into the mirror of God's word and find
Our God has ever been faithful and never late.
We trust in the Lord, as the Word of God extols.
Like Job we wait until at last our change shall come,
Assured that in patience we now anchor our souls.
May we not faint and fall by the wayside as some
But follow in Christ's steps, as we quickly obey
And bear up under and yield fruit of endurance.
We must walk in God's love, the more excellent way
And through faith and patience claim our inheritance.
In these perilous times we remain yielded and still,
Watching, waiting, seeking to fulfill all of God's will.

2

WATCHMAN: WATCH YOUR MOUTH AND OTHER MATTERS

Watch the way you talk. Let nothing foul or dirty come out of your mouth. Say only what helps, each word a gift.

–Ephesians 4:29 (Message Bible)

My strategy for overcoming an adverse situation, such as a physical condition like prostate cancer, involves going to the Bible to see what it has to say about the issue in question. The next step involves observing how the scriptures I found apply to me and my attempts to deal with the situation confronting me. Without question, the Word of God is practical and is profitable, as we note in 2 Timothy 3:16-17 (New Living Translation):

> All scripture is inspired by God and is useful to teach us what is true and to make us realize what is wrong in our lives. It corrects us when we are wrong and teaches us to do what is right.

God uses it to prepare and equip His people to do every good work.

The first step of my response to prostate cancer was *to watch*. Throughout the scriptures, I found references to this verb *watch*. The Old Testament speaks of the importance of watches and watchmen. The period of time between sunset and sunrise was divided into watches where watchmen relieved one another during these intervals. Originally, there were three watches of the night: "the beginning of the watches," "the middle watch" and "the morning watch." The New Testament mentions four watches, with a new segment probably introduced by the Romans. Mark 13:35 (New King James Version) makes reference to four such watchful periods:

> Watch therefore, for you do not know when the master of the house is coming--in the evening, at midnight, at the crowing of the rooster, or in the morning—

One of the primary duties of those who watch or watchmen was to sound the alarm of an approaching enemy observed from watch-towers. Note this passage from Isaiah 21:5-7 (NLT):

> Look! They are preparing a great feast.
>   They are spreading rugs for people to sit on.
>   Everyone is eating and drinking.
> But quick! Grab your shields and prepare for battle.
>   You are being attacked!
> ⁶ Meanwhile, the Lord said to me,
> "Put a watchman on the city wall.
>   Let him shout out what he sees.
> ⁷ He should look for chariots
>   drawn by pairs of horses,
> and for riders on donkeys and camels.
>   Let the watchman be fully alert.

Similarly, I needed to set watchmen on the walls of my life so I could be aware when the enemy is coming to attack my body, mind, or any other area of my life.

Throughout the Gospels, Jesus Christ also speaks regarding *watch* as a command to his followers—"And what I say unto you I say unto all, Watch (Mark 13:37)." In addition, *watch and pray* is a familiar exhortation from the Gospels where Jesus exhorts the disciples—"Watch and pray, lest you enter not into temptation. The spirit indeed is willing, but the flesh is weak (Matthew 26:41)." Concerning Jesus Christ's return, he also tells his disciples in Mark 13:33 (NKJV)—"Take heed, watch and pray; for you do not know when the time is."

He also goes on to encourage them regarding the same topic in Luke 21:36—"Watch therefore, and pray always that you may be counted worthy to escape all these things that will come to pass, and to stand before the Son of Man."

In the letters written by Paul, a similar combination of these two verbs is found in Colossians 4:2 (King James Version)—"Continue earnestly in prayer, and watch in the same with thanksgiving." At the end of I Corinthians 16, Paul reminds us in verse 13—"Watch, stand fast in the faith, be brave, be strong." He continues in Ephesians 6:18—"Praying always with all prayer and supplication in the Spirit, and watching thereunto with all perseverance and supplication for all saints;"

In I Thessalonians after the comforting words regarding Christ's return in Chapter 5, verses 6–8, Paul goes on to encourage the believers with these words:

> Therefore let us not sleep, as do others; but let us watch and be sober.
> For those who sleep, sleep at night, and those who get drunk are drunk at night.
> But let us, who are of the day, be sober, putting on the breastplate of faith and love, and as a helmet, the hope of salvation.

WATCHMAN

This final reminder comes from 1 Peter 4:7—"But the end of all things is at hand: therefore be serious and watchful in your prayers."

In response to having received the diagnosis of prostate cancer, I found three areas of my personal life I had to monitor or closely watch. Because these areas impacted me in such a profound way and influenced the decisions I made, I recognized I had to become a guardian or watchman of what John Bunyan calls "every gate that opens in our heart." Morgan speaks of gates in this way—"They are the places that we have to monitor diligently so that we allow only that which is positive and healthy into our lives." Three such gates are the ear gate, the eye gate, and the mouth gate. The picture of the three wise monkeys came to mind to remind me that I must consciously seek to "watch what I hear, watch what I see, and watch what I say."

I found simple words of encouragement to follow these directives in some of the lyrics to a children's ministry song—*Oh, Be Careful Little Eyes*:

> O be careful little eyes what you see
> O be careful little eyes what you see
> There's a Father up above
> And He's looking down in love
> So, be careful little eyes what you see
>
> O be careful little ears what you hear
> O be careful little ears what you hear
> There's a Father up above
> And He's looking down in love
> So, be careful little ears what you hear
>
> O be careful little mouth what you say
> O be careful little mouth what you say
> There's a Father up above

EMBRACING YOUR LIFE SENTENCE

And He's looking down in love
So, be careful little mouth what you say

WATCH YOUR EARS

Whenever it was possible, I consciously and consistently made every effort to listen to words and music that edified and encouraged rather than tore down and destroyed. My favorite kinds of music are inspired by the Word of God in a whole range of categories, from classical music to hymns and gospel music, both traditional as well as contemporary praise, and worship. I especially enjoy instrumental music, such as jazz with a Christian flavor. With song lyrics, I made a concerted effort to listen for words of life and hope, for as K. Eubanks noted, "It is faith that breathes life into hope."

Positive generates positive, while negative produces negative, as I learned to listen attentively that I might not only hear but also understand. During the early stages of my diagnosis, I listened to many teachings about healing. I had previously shared the Word of God regarding faith and other related areas, and I listened to recordings of these messages over and over.

Consciously and consistently I had to place my ears near to the lips of God, as I attempted to perfect the art of listening. Proverbs 8:34 speaks of the blessing that comes to the individual who watches and waits on the Lord—

> Blessed is the man that hears me, watching daily at my gates, waiting at the posts of my doors.

WATCH YOUR EYES

In response to questions from his companions, Job makes this statement—"I made a covenant with mine eyes. . . " Without question, I realized my mind can be flooded with negative images of all sorts, but I can choose instead to focus my attention on the positive. Similarly, I chose to dwell upon positive mental images rather than negative ones. I had previously made use of visualization techniques to see myself successfully completing tasks set before me, such as successfully completing a rigorous interview with the desired results or teaching or learning a new teaching technique. I recalled the words of Paul J. Meyer—"Whatever you vividly imagine, ardently desire, sincerely believe, and enthusiastically act upon, must inevitably come to pass."

I remained confident I would get through the critical situation that confronted me and come through it triumphantly. I always kept this picture of success in my mind's eye as I read and confessed the Word of God.

Watch Your Mouth

Concerning the mouth as a gate that I had to watch, I had to monitor what went into the mouth as well as what came out of my mouth—what I chose to eat and what I chose to speak. When I was first diagnosed with prostate cancer, I was determined to modify my diet and eliminate red meat and other foods that could possibly contribute to the growth of cancer. I also began to take a combination of herbs along with vitamins, minerals, and other remedies. Later, in implementing my strategy, I would also watch my urinary pH to make sure it was above seven (or alkaline), as opposed to below seven (acidic), an environment wherein cancer cells thrive.

Moreover, I watched my mouth in this way. Ephesians 4:29 in the Message Bible reveals what I did:

> Watch the way you talk. Let nothing foul or dirty come out of your mouth. Say only what helps, each word a gift.

EMBRACING YOUR LIFE SENTENCE

Since "The power of life and death is in the power of the tongue," according to Proverbs 18:21, I carefully chose the words I would speak, as this original poem states:

> We know the tongue has power to generate life,
> To produce seeds that will eventually take root
> And will bring forth two very different kinds of fruit:
> Love, joy and peace or envy, confusion and strife
> Can build or destroy a brother, a friend, a wife.

Throughout the whole process of responding to the diagnosis of prostate cancer, I had to encourage myself to make positive confessions and speak words of positive affirmation. The scriptures remind believers to let our words always be seasoned with salt, that they may minister grace to the hearers.

I was amazed I did not have to look in the mirror to watch my mouth, but then again, I did! I looked into the mirror of the Word of God and made sure what I said lined up with what the Word of God says. The Book of James speaks of not only being one who hears the Word but also one who does the Word—"a hearer *and* a doer." Indeed, my actions spoke louder than my words in this instance.

To sum up what I learned about watching strategically, I came across this statement attributed to Frank Outlaw, founder of Bi-Lo Stores. Each line opens with an exhortation to *watch*. What we are to observe closely could be arranged as an acrostic to spell W-A-T-C-H:

> Watch your thoughts, they become words;
> watch your words, they become actions;
> watch your actions, they become habits;
> watch your habits, they become character;
> watch your character, for it becomes your destiny.

Watchful Waiting

My specific response to the initial diagnosis of cancer was that I chose to follow the protocol of watchful waiting. Since prostate cancer generally grows slowly, I decided not to undergo any of the more radical treatment alternatives, such as prostatectomy or surgically removing the prostate gland, which can result in incontinence and impotence. Other options were presented to me: radiation therapy, cryotherapy—freezing the prostate and then removing it—or, I could directly monitor the PSA levels and have a physical examination of the prostate on a more regular basis. I thought of one of the stanzas from one of my favorite hymns, *Blessed Assurance*, which captures the essence of this approach for me:

> Watching and waiting, looking above,
> Filled with His goodness, lost in His love.

Each chapter of *Embracing Your Life Sentence: How to Turn Life's Greatest Tragedies into Your Greatest Triumphs* concludes with a psalm of remembrance of God's goodness and faithfulness. As the journey continues, I am a—

Watchman, Watchman on the Wall

Watchman, watchman on the wall keep your eyes on the Eastern skies
Until the thickened darkness flees and the daystar shall arise.
Consecrate yourself and keep your ears near to the lips of God,
Waiting, anticipating, responding to the voice of God.

Your steps are ordered to walk in humility, as the wise,
To covenant with the Lord and serve Him, as you fix your eyes

EMBRACING YOUR LIFE SENTENCE

On the prize and press toward the mark of the high calling of God,
Watchman, watchman on the wall.

Attend to the Word of the Lord you hear and see how it applies
To your life. Let it speak: become the message you recognize.
Position yourself to occupy the atmosphere with God.
Know that you are far more than you are now says the Lord, your God,
Watchman, watchman on the wall.

3

FIGHTER: THE FIGHT OF MY LIFE, THE FIGHT FOR MY LIFE

Receiving my prostate cancer diagnosis was like hearing the bell announcing round one of the fight of my life, as well as the fight for my life.

The second phase of my three-fold strategy centered on aspects of the soul—the mind, will, and emotions—as I examined the powerful action verb *to fight*. John Eldredge speaks of "a battle to fight," an essential quality of being a man in *Wild at Heart*, a life-changing book that ministered to the core of who I am and who I aspire to be. Eldredge indicates three motivational factors expressing the essence of manhood, describing a man who is ever seeking "a battle to fight," "an adventure to live" and "a beauty to rescue." In thinking about these three primary driving forces of men, I recognized that life is a battlefield, and the battlefield is the mind. Although I had been aware of this most of my adult life, I really came to grips with the intensity of a battle to fight when I was diagnosed with prostate cancer in 2000.

Throughout the scriptures, there are many references to the verb *fight*.

EMBRACING YOUR LIFE SENTENCE

In 1 Timothy 6:12 (NKJV), Paul speaks about fighting:

> Fight the good fight of faith, lay hold on eternal life, to which you were also called and have confessed a good confession in the presence of many witnesses.

I thought of other scriptures related to fighting in those instances where the Lord fights for us. The passage from Exodus where the Children of Israel confront the Red Sea in their escape from Egypt also came to mind, from Exodus 14:14 (NKJV):

> The LORD will fight for you, and you shall hold your peace.

A similar exhortation came from Deuteronomy 20:4 (NKJV):

> For the LORD your God is He who goes with you, to fight for you against your enemies, to save you.

We are reminded of the same truth in Joshua 23:10:

> [10] Each one of you will put to flight a thousand of the enemy, for the LORD YOUR GOD FIGHTS FOR YOU, JUST AS HE HAS PROMISED.

We find wonderful words of encouragement from David in Psalm 144:1–2:

> Blessed be the LORD my Rock,
> Who trains my hands for war,
> And my fingers for battle—
> My lovingkindness and my fortress, My high tower and my deliverer,

FIGHTER

My shield, and *the One* in whom I take refuge,
Who subdues my people under me.

In the early days of my diagnosis, I watched the completion of the Olympic Games during the summer of 2004, and I thought of a reference to *fight* from one of my most cherished passages, the athletic analogy from I Corinthians 9:24–27 (NKJV):

> Do you not know that those who run in a race all run, but one receives the prize? Run in such a way that you may obtain *it*.
> And everyone who competes *for the prize* is temperate in all things.
> Now they *do it* to obtain a perishable crown, but we *for* an imperishable *crown*.
> Therefore I run thus: not with uncertainty. Thus I fight: not as *one who* beats the air.
> But I discipline my body and bring *it* into subjection, lest, when I have preached to others, I myself should become disqualified.

I learned firsthand the fight we are in is real, and we are not only shadow-boxing. I recognized, however, we must "endure a great fight of afflictions" as mentioned in Hebrews. We have already won, but we merely need to finish the course. Then, we will be able to believe as Paul did in II Timothy 4:7–8:

> I have fought the good fight, I have finished the race, I have kept the faith: Finally, there is laid up for me the crown of righteousness, which the Lord, the righteous judge, will give to me on that Day: and not to me only but also all who have loved His appearing.

EMBRACING YOUR LIFE SENTENCE

THE REAL BATTLEFIELD IS THE MIND

In the arena of spiritual warfare, the real battlefield is the mind. This message is most clearly and concisely expressed in II Corinthians 10:3–5:

> For though we walk in the flesh, we do not war according to the flesh. For the weapons of our warfare are not carnal but mighty in God for pulling down strongholds, Casting down arguments and every high thing that exalts itself against the knowledge of God, bringing every thought into captivity to the obedience of Christ,

In verse 5, "casting down," as used in the New Testament, means "to take down (as from a higher place) with the idea of force to pull down, demolish, while arguments is a variation of the same verb form, meaning "demolition, extinction—destruction, pulling down."

I recognized in the early stages of the disease that I was in the fight of my life. As David ran toward Goliath to defeat that monstrous giant with a single shot from his sling, I learned to move forward aggressively, putting off old thinking patterns and putting on new ways of thinking, based on the scriptures, as part of the continuing process called renewing of the mind, an essential element of the winning strategy to defeat prostate cancer.

Paul referenced this ongoing practice every believer must engage in every moment of every day while we draw breath. Romans 12:2 addresses this transformative process, from The Amplified Bible:

> ² And do not be conformed to this world [any longer with its superficial values and customs], but be transformed *and* progressively changed [as you mature spiritually] by the renewing of your mind [focusing on godly values and ethical attitudes], so that you may prove [for yourselves]

FIGHTER

what the will of God is, that which is good and acceptable and perfect [in His plan and purpose for you].

For most of the years of my adult life as a believer, I recognized the importance of the opening verses of Romans 12 and committed this passage to memory. In my understanding of these verses, I thought of the renewed mind as something believers had to obtain or lay hold of. Later, I read the passage more closely and recognized the reference emphasized the renewing of the mind—an active, ongoing process.

This section of scripture is associated with the familiar process of metamorphosis butterflies and other organisms undergo. Christians are instructed not to be conformed but to be transformed by the renewing of their minds. The New Testament phrase is translated from the Greek word from which the English word metamorphosis is derived. The phrase is also used to express that as believers strive to manifest more of Christ in their lives, they are also changed into the same image through this ongoing course of action.

Butterflies as they undergo metamorphosis are transformed from egg to larva or caterpillar to chrysalis (cocoon) to butterfly (adult). Christian believers also continually undergo a similar spiritual transformation as they mature in Christ. The essence of this amazing process is expressed in the poem, *Death to the Caterpillar*, and in John 12:24:

> Most assuredly, I say to you, unless a grain of wheat falls into the ground and dies, it remains alone; but if it dies, it produces much grain.
> *John 12:24*

What is death to the caterpillar we call a butterfly.

—Anonymous

Death to the Caterpillar

> From the dark of earth new life stems from seeds once sown.
> Despite the pain of loss and our questioning why,
> From the source of life this eternal truth is shown:
> "Death to the caterpillar we call a butterfly."
> Creation travails until the sons of God appear;
> No longer conformed, we have at last been set free,
> As every Kingdom mystery is now made clear,
> Totally transformed into glorious liberty.
> Triumphant in the race we desired to win:
> From victory to victory and glory to glory,
> We see that power to change comes from within,
> As we write another chapter of our life's story.
> The final stage of glory unfolds this result:
> Transformed from egg to larva to pupa to adult.

The process of renewing the mind is constant, as each day becomes a challenge to put off the old man—those old negative thinking patterns—and to put on the new man—those positive thoughts based on the Word of God. This concept is also referred to as putting on the mind of Christ, and each individual rises to success or failure in the battlefield of the mind.

Without question, I learned that renewing the mind or changing my thought patterns is an active and aggressive activity, as I had to seize control of my thoughts and emotions. Never was I more aware of the importance of controlling my thoughts by putting on the mind of Christ—dispelling the negative thoughts that defeat the promises of God.

In my efforts to understand more fully the intense internal struggles confronting me, I recognized the conflicts that rage within each believer: the ongoing battle between good and evil and the constant struggle between fulfilling the lusts of the flesh and walking by the spirit.

Throughout this entire process of renewing the mind, I recognized the internal conflict was real, as I seemed to be waging war at times for my sanity. I was certainly more aware of the these intense inner struggles following my diagnosis of prostate cancer. I recall thinking of the lyrics to the familiar hymn, *Just As I Am*, which speaks of internal and external struggles:

> Just as I am, though tossed about
> with many a conflict, many a doubt,
> fightings and fears within, without,
> O Lamb of God, I come, I come.

These lyrics echo the sentiments expressed by Paul who speaks of his desire to come to the believers in Macedonia when he says, "our flesh had no rest, but we were troubled on every side; without were fightings, within were fears."

Galatians 5: 16-18 in the Amplified Bible sharply delineate this dilemma:

> [16] But I say, walk *and* live [habitually] in the [Holy] Spirit [responsive to *and* controlled *and* guided by the Spirit]; then you will certainly not gratify the cravings *and* desires of the flesh (of human nature without God).

> [17] For the desires of the flesh are opposed to the [Holy] Spirit, and the [desires of the] Spirit are opposed to the flesh (godless human nature); for these are antagonistic to each other [continually withstanding and in conflict with each other], so that you are not free *but* are prevented from doing what you desire to do.

> [18] But if you are guided (led) by the [Holy] Spirit, you are not subject to the Law.

EMBRACING YOUR LIFE SENTENCE

Paul goes on to draw a sharp contrast between the works of the flesh and the fruit of the spirit.

This never-ending internal conflict is also depicted in Romans 7:18-25, where Paul speaks of his desire to do good, but he winds up doing the very thing that he doesn't want to do, and regrettably he does not do what he so longs to do.

> For I know that in me (that is, in my flesh) nothing good dwells; for to will is present with me, but *how* to perform what is good I do not find.
>
> [19] For the good that I will *to do,* I do not do; but the evil I will not *to do,* that I practice.
>
> [20] Now if I do what I will not *to do,* it is no longer I who do it, but sin that dwells in me.
>
> [21] I find then a law, that evil is present with me, the one who wills to do good.
>
> [22] For I delight in the law of God according to the inward man.
>
> [23] But I see another law in my members, warring against the law of my mind, and bringing me into captivity to the law of sin which is in my members.
>
> [24] O wretched man that I am! Who will deliver me from this body of death?
>
> [25] I thank God—through Jesus Christ our Lord!
>
> So then, with the mind I myself serve the law of God, but with the flesh the law of sin.

FIGHTER

During the time of my internal struggles to get it together and keep it together, I was teaching a class on American literature, and one of the writers whom we discussed was Colonial poet Anne Bradstreet (1612-1672), who personalized the constant conflict raging within her own mind and within every Christian believer in an excerpt from *The Flesh and the Spirit*:

> I heard two sisters reason on
> Things that are past and things to come.
> One Flesh was call'd, who had her eye
> On worldly wealth and vanity;
> The other Spirit, who did rear
> Her thoughts unto a higher sphere.

This intense internal conflict is depicted in my original poem as a fight where each individual can determine the outcome:

Two Ravenous Wolves

An elder Cherokee chief took his grandchildren
into the forest and sat them down and said to them,
'A fight is going on inside me. This is a terrible fight
and it is a fight between two wolves.
One wolf is the wolf of fear, anger, arrogance and greed.
The other wolf is the wolf of courage, kindness,
humility and love. . . . This same fight between the
two wolves that is going on inside of me
is going on inside of you, and inside every person.
                              —Rabbi Marc Gellman

Two ravenous wolves wage constant warfare within.
Each stalks the other, striving to survive, to reign.
One embodies fear, anger, arrogance, and greed,
The other courage, kindness, humility and love:

One a sinister serpent, one a gentle dove.
Each tries to gain the upper hand and to restrain
Its foe, but only one will rise to seize the lead.
Each is seeking to dominate, driven to gain.
One will be defeated--only one will remain.
Since each beast demands the opposite kind of food,
We select the diet, whether evil or good.
In each conflict, the soul determines who will win,
For wolves are ravaged by an all-consuming need,
And we decide the wolf we starve, the wolf we feed.

Overcoming Toxic Emotions

A deep internal cleansing or detoxing of the body can be part of the strategy some individuals choose to undergo when they have cancer. Similarly, some patients may need an emotional detox program to overcome toxic emotions, which can negatively impact the body's response to cancer. In discussing the concept of renewing the mind, Bishop Charles Mellette speaks of managing your mind: "You have to renew your mind to manage your thoughts (pictures of the mind that have constructive possibilities that affect your life, positively and negatively)."

Two Ravenous Wolves referenced many dangerous emotions, which if unchecked or not countered, can precipitate a destructive downward spiral that can sabotage the destiny of a believer. Another related poem also lists additional negative emotions that can have devastating consequences:

Dangerous Emotions

We capture their rebellious thoughts and teach them to obey Christ.
—2 Corinthians 10:5b

FIGHTER

As the champions of God, ministers of the Word,
We must overcome each dangerous emotion.
As we fight the good fight, using our shield and sword,
Clothed with the whole armor, not seeking promotion
Of ourselves but of the Savior, who gave His life,
An example that we should follow in His steps,
That we might slay giants of fear, envy and strife.
Stubborn rebellion that would defy God's precepts
And defile desire to serve Him in purity,
We defeat with a smooth stone of obedience.
Resentment, guilt, anger and green-eyed jealousy:
Each toxic emotion yields deadly consequence.
Pride, described as the most dangerous of them all,
Leads to destruction and goes before a downfall.

In critical situations where a person may have accidentally ingested a highly toxic substance, the state poison control center, if contacted, can suggest a specific antidote to counteract that poison. In some cases, a universal antidote is recommended. Activated charcoal has the well-earned reputation of being such an antidote since it can facilitate the removal of many poisonous substances before they can cause harm. In the case of some of the toxic emotions previously discussed, another universal antidote is recommended to counteract any and all of these negative issues of life. A heavy dose of thanksgiving will counter the potentially crippling negative effects of resentment, guilt, anger, and green-eyed jealousy along with fear, envy, and strife, all of which are aggravated by stubborn rebellion, which generates these toxic emotions.

When most people hear the term thanksgiving, there is an almost automatic association with turkey, dressing, cranberries, and pumpkin pie (or sweet potato pie, depending upon your ethnic tastes). Many associate the word with pageants of Pilgrims and Native Americans, with parades and football games—the prelude to the final holiday season of the year. For many people around the world, however, thanksgiving is more than a holiday observed the fourth Thursday in November. Actually, thanksgiving is *always* appropriate. Thanksgiving should be the reason for every season.

Let me first of all explain exactly what I mean by thanksgiving. In its most basic sense, thanksgiving is the application of an essential principle of life: giving and receiving. When one gives, one receives, and always in higher proportion than one gives. Although many people think of giving and receiving in terms of tithes and offerings or of giving of material abundance within a church or religious context, the universal principle works in all aspects of life—particularly in thanksgiving, most literally to give thanks or to show oneself grateful. The term expresses gratitude, a form of prayer specified in I Timothy 2:1: ". . . requests, prayers, intercession and thanksgiving. . . ."

As Christian believers, giving thanks to God for His grace and goodness reverses the negative thinking pattern generated by toxic emotions. I learned I cannot honestly be thankful and feel fearful or disappointed at the same time, nor can I be angry nor discouraged when I see all God has done for me and express gratitude to Him at the same time. Indeed, I cannot simultaneously sink to the depths of despair when I recognize how blessed I have been thus far, as I anticipate even greater blessings on the horizon, for the best is always yet to come with God, my beneficent Father.

God wants us to show ourselves grateful at all times. The Word of God reminds us of this truth in several places:

Colossians 3:17—

> And whatever you do, whether in word or deed, do it all in the name of the Lord Jesus, giving thanks to God the Father through him.

Ephesians 5:20—

> Always giving thanks to God the Father for everything, in the name of our Lord Jesus Christ.

The Word of God reveals that the giving of thanks is to be more than an occasional act of gratitude; it is to be an ongoing part of our lives.

Philippians 4:6—

> Do not be anxious about anything, but in everything, by prayer and petition, with thanksgiving, present your requests to *God*.

Hebrews 13:15—

> By him therefore let us offer the sacrifice of praise to God continually, that is, the fruit of our lips giving thanks to his name. KJV

Perhaps the most dramatic reminder to live in continuous thanksgiving is found in I Thessalonians 5:18.

The King James Version renders the verse this way—

> In everything give thanks: for this is the will of God in Christ Jesus concerning you.

To facilitate memorizing this particular verse, I composed a scripture Memory Song, *In Everything Give Thanks*:

> In everything give thanks,
> In everything give thanks,
> For this is the will of God
> In Christ Jesus concerning you.

EMBRACING YOUR LIFE SENTENCE

Repeat

When things in life don't seem to turn out
Just as we think they should,
We know that God still has a grand plan
And works all things together—
He works all things together for our good.

In everything give thanks,
In everything give thanks,
For this is the will of God
In Christ Jesus concerning you.

The sun shines bright or the darkest night,
No matter what the mood,
We still give thanks always for all things.
In the name of Jesus Christ,
We keep an attitude of gratitude.

In everything give thanks,
In everything give thanks,
For this is the will of God
In Christ Jesus concerning you.

Every situation offers an opportunity to be thankful, no matter how bright or bleak life may be. If I think about it, I can always find something to be thankful for, if for nothing more than that I am alive or that my situation could be worse. I can begin with thanking God that I am alive and then adding to the long list of blessings I am enjoying at that moment. Each time I set my mind to be thankful, I am doing the will of God, which is the innermost desire of every believer. To give thanks is to do the will of God.

Feeling disappointed, discouraged, and in despair or having other negative feelings is sometimes described as stinkin' thinkin', which directly affects how I act. One of the critical factors in my physical and emotional well-being is my attitude. Chuck Swindoll offers excellent insight regarding this subject:

> The longer I live, the more I realize the impact of attitude on life. Attitude, to me, is more important than facts. It is more important than the past, than education, than money, than circumstances, than failures, than successes, than what other people think or say or do. It is more important than appearance, giftedness, or skill. It will make or break a company...a church... a home.
>
> The remarkable thing is we have a choice every day regarding the attitude we will embrace for that day. We cannot change our past... we cannot change the fact that people will act in a certain way. We cannot change the inevitable. The only thing we can do is play on the one string we have, and that is our attitude...I am convinced that life is 10% what happens to me and 90% how I react to it. And so it is with you...we are in charge of our Attitudes.

The discussion of attitude comes full circle with a reminder that attitude begins with gratitude. J. Rufus Moseley speaks of "an attitude of gratitude and boundless goodwill." Thanksgiving is a magnificent and joyful response-ability, that is, my ability to *respond* to God's love and grace. As a believer, I continually endeavor to demonstrate my gratitude to God from the fullness of my heart, overflowing with thanks. More than merely occasionally expressing how grateful I am, I desire to maintain a continual attitude of gratitude, a lifestyle that some have called *thanksliving*. The essence of my attitude of endless gratitude is expressed through poetry:

Thanksliving

What shall I render to the Lord for all
His grace? What can I say to offer praise
Worthy of His glory? How can I call
With all my being upon His name and raise
A new song from the depths of my heart?
I must do more than mouth a platitude—
To express the soul in words is an art;
Yet words cannot express my gratitude.
Mere words seem empty and without merit.
"Thank you" too soon becomes a hollow phrase.
So I must worship God with my spirit
And must give thanks well for all of my days.
To live is give thanks with tongue and limb;
With each breath, each move, I must *live* thanks to Him.

Far more than merely saying "thank you" to God, more than simply tithing or sharing of our abundance or giving of our time or material goods, *thanksliving* is a way of life, expressing gratitude to God in everything we say and do. It is more than the arrival of Friday (TGIF), for which the workaday world thanks God. I found out that I must show how grateful I am with all of my being—"Thank God it's Sunday through Saturday." As I do so, I counteract the negative effects of disappointment, discouragement, despair, and any other toxic emotions that keep me from being all that God designed me to be.

In reflecting on this particular phase of my journey with prostate cancer, I recalled a statement by Donald Lawrence which provided an introduction to the following:

FIGHTER

In the Fight for My Life

God will keep it together until you get it together.
                                      —Donald Lawrence

In the fight for my life,
I asked God, my Father, to help me
Get it together and keep it together
God answered and strengthened me
So that I could weather any storm
God kept it together
Until I got it together

No matter what happened,
I kept on watching and waiting
With outstretched neck,
Yearning, ever anticipating
Until Christ returns to gather us together

Until then. . .
In the fight for my life,
I continue to tell myself
Get it together and keep it together
It won't be long.

On countless occasions following my diagnosis of prostate cancer I woke up and began my day with grateful praise to God to see another day. I thanked the Lord that I was clothed in my right mind. As I acknowledged I had so much to be thankful for, and as I reflected upon the goodness of God, I thought of Psalm 124, a psalm of David—a song for pilgrims ascending to Jerusalem—which I would read aloud in the New Living Translation. Here the Psalmist stimulated my thinking with one of those "What if?" questions:

EMBRACING YOUR LIFE SENTENCE

¹ What if the L ORD HAD NOT BEEN ON OUR SIDE?
  Let all Israel repeat:
² What if the L ORD HAD NOT BEEN ON OUR SIDE
  when people attacked us?
³ They would have swallowed us alive
  in their burning anger.
⁴ The waters would have engulfed us;
  a torrent would have overwhelmed us.
⁵ Yes, the raging waters of their fury
  would have overwhelmed our very lives.
⁶ Praise the L ORD,
  who did not let their teeth tear us apart!
⁷ We escaped like a bird from a hunter's trap.
  The trap is broken, and we are free!
⁸ Our help is from the L ORD,
  who made heaven and earth.

⁶ Praise the Lord,
  who did not let their teeth tear us apart!

Verse 1 in the King James Version was the inspiration for my personal poetic conclusions on fighting for my life:

If It Had Not Been for the Lord

If it had not been the LORD who was on our side,
Let Israel now say—
                                          —Psalm 124:1

If it had not been for the Lord who was on my side,
I would have drowned in the sea from the tears I cried.
I shudder to think just where I would be today.
I would have lost my mind or turned and walked away,
But I learned that God is faithful—this cannot be denied.

FIGHTER

He was there to guide when I was tempted and tried,
My shelter from the storm where I could run and hide.
He was my deliverer—that is all I have to say:
If it had not been for the Lord.

Enemies rose up like a flood to wash aside,
But God came through and rescued me and turned the tide.
Pressing toward the mark, dawning of a brand new day,
Through all my trials I learned to watch, fight and pray.
The Lord is my keeper; in Him I confide:
If it had not been for the Lord.

4

PRAYER WARRIOR: DEMONSTRATING THE POWER OF PRAYER

There is always something to pray about. As with the physical and emotional aspects of being diagnosed with prostate cancer, I also focused on the spiritual dimension related to my situation. From the onset, I began to pray as never before. I combined the action verbs fight and pray in my designation as a prayer warrior who recognized the power of prayer. With the Word of God as my primary resource, I examined different kinds of prayer as essential components of my relationship with God through Jesus Christ in whose name I pray.

In its purest form, prayer is communication with God. For the Christian believer, however, this conversation should not always lapse into a monologue of personal petitions. Brother Lawrence reminds us, prayer is a unique privilege—"There is not in the world a kind of life more sweet and delightful than that of a continual conversation with God." Indeed, prayer should be ongoing in every Christian believer.

The Bible reveals many kinds of prayer which are the bedrock of our relationship with God through Jesus Christ in whose name we pray. 1 Timothy 2:1 introduces 4 types of prayer or ways of communing with God:

> I exhort therefore, that, first of all, supplications, prayers, intercessions, and giving of thanks, be made for all men.

In reflecting on how my prayer life continued to unfold during the time of my diagnosis of prostate cancer, I recognize all four types of prayer were involved to varying degrees.

SUPPLICATIONS

With these prayers, we entreat our Father with specific requests. Such petitions focus on our necessity expressed as a personal need, rather than God's sufficiency to supply it. White-hot zeal and insatiable hunger ignite prayers of supplication. Strictly speaking, supplication also conveys an accompanying attitude of prayer, noting the "the effectual fervent prayer of a righteous man avails much (James 5:16)." I was passionately praying on my own behalf during my encounter with cancer.

INTERCESSIONS

To intercede means to plead or mediate on behalf of another person. Intercession will involve meeting with someone on behalf of someone else. Those who act as intercessors are also described as *standing in the gap* or *making up the hedge* which provide protection, according to Ezekiel 22:30. Throughout the time of my health challenges, believers in my church community and elsewhere were also interceding for me.

PRAYERS

As we acknowledge the magnitude of God, we offer prayers as an expression of our personal devotion. Other examples included in this category are the prayers of faith, agreement, and dedication or consecration; also the prayer Jesus taught his disciples or *The Lord's Prayer*. Paul reminds believers in Ephesians 6:18 to be "praying always with all prayer and supplication in the Spirit, being watchful to this end with all perseverance and supplication for all the saints."

THANKSGIVING

Thanksgiving should be an essential part of our ongoing conversation with God. It means to give of thanks as an expression of showing oneself grateful. It is an all-encompassing attitude of gratitude involving everything we do and say—"In everything give thanks, for this is the will of God in Christ Jesus concerning you (I Thessalonians 5:18)." This kind of prayer will be discussed in more detail later in this chapter.

Since the late 1960s when I developed a closer personal relationship with Jesus Christ while serving in the US Army, I have recognized that praying is an essential part of my Christian walk. In reading the Gospels, I learned that Jesus established a pattern in Mark 1:35—"In the morning, rising up a great while before day he went out into a solitary place and there prayed." I decided to develop a similar habit pattern of praying when I first got up in the morning, often before sunrise. Throughout the day, I tried to set aside time to pray for situations that individuals had asked me to pray about, for personal needs, or to thank God for His blessings. I also prayed as the day ended, often with my wife or alone as I reflected on the day with gratitude to God.

During the time after receiving my diagnosis of prostate cancer, I kept a prayer journal/scrapbook in which I posted scriptures, poems, song lyrics, quotations, personal prophetic words, photographs, maps, and other items I used daily as touchstones in my time of prayer. Among the scriptures relating to prayer are I Thessalonians 5:17, 18, 25:

Pray without ceasing. In everything give thanks, for this is the will of God in Christ Jesus for you.

Brethren, pray for us.
Luke 18:1b reminds us that "men ought always to pray and not lose heart." In addition, I composed a scripture memory song that I would sing from time to time:

We ought always to pray and not to faint.
We ought always to pray and not to faint.
We ought always to pray and not to faint.
To pray, pray, pray, pray, pray without ceasing

II Thessalonians 3:1-5 offers this powerful exhortation:

Finally, brethren, pray for us, that the word of the Lord may run *swiftly* and be glorified, just as *it is* with you,

And that we may be delivered from unreasonable and wicked men; for not all have faith.

But the Lord is faithful, who will establish you and guard *you* from the evil one.

And we have confidence in the Lord concerning you, both that you do and will do the things we command you.

Now may the Lord direct your hearts into the love of God and into the patience of Christ.

These scriptures all related to prayer, and most were part of my prayer journal/scrapbook. One of the original statements I made over the years regarding prayer is this—*There is always something to pray about.* My diagnosis was one more item on my ongoing list of concerns to pray about or as Pastor Jean

Oscar Njock Bayiha, my friend from Dakar Senegal, calls them, "prayer topics." In the days following my diagnosis, my physical, mental or emotional, and spiritual well-being was certainly on my list of concerns I prayed for.

CRAFTED PRAYER: PERFECTING THE ART

In his book *Crafted Prayer: The Joy of Always Getting Your Prayers Answered,* Bible teacher Graham Cooke shows how to use the scriptures to construct specific, targeted prayers, addressed to God offered individually as well as corporately. Cook maintains that crafted prayer is designed so those who pray will know "the joy of always getting your prayers answered." The Bible offers this assurance to those who pray the Word of God in Isaiah 55:11—

> So shall my word be that goes forth from my mouth; it shall not return unto me void, but it shall accomplish what I please and it shall prosper in the thing to which I sent it.

I John 5:14-15 also reminds us—

> [14]And this is the confidence that we have in him, that, if we ask any thing according to his will, he hears us: [15]And if we know that he hears us, whatever we ask, we know that we have the petitions that we desired of him.

Crafted prayers are like handcrafted arrows, works of art within themselves, designed to be on target consistently. Jeremiah described the nations who attacked Babylon in this way—"Their arrows *shall be* like *those* of an expert warrior; none shall return in vain (Jeremiah 50:9)." Similarly, crafted prayers are exquisitely designed and accurately dispatched to specific targets, and they always hit the mark.

PRAYER WARRIOR

Prayer has been described as a powerful offensive weapon in the spiritual arsenal of believers. The illustration and application of crafted prayer as arrows provides a picture of how prayer can be used offensively with precision to a limited degree. In light of how modern warfare has changed as we have moved further into the 21st Century, a more precise revision of the original analogy would take us from arrows to smart-bombs released with pinpoint laser accuracy.

In an article in the *LA Times*, Peter Pae writes about lasers and their use in modern warfare:

> The word 'laser' is an acronym that stands for 'light amplification by stimulated emission of radiation.' The technology turns atomic particles into light with enough radiation to damage an object it encounters.
>
> The range and severity of the damage depend on how much power can be generated and how well the light can be focused on the target.
>
> . . . [L]aser scientists say significant technical challenges recently have been overcome, transforming laser weapons from a laboratory project into a promising part of the U.S. arsenal. With such lasers, a fighter jet could destroy ground targets with pinpoint accuracy, significantly reducing the chance of injuring civilians.

A passage from Ephesians 6:10-18 reminds believers of the power of prayer, used as an offensive weapon in the ongoing spiritual battle called life. For the Christian believer, putting on the whole armor of God should apply to every situation, but this passage had particular application to my specific situation regarding cancer, especially the last verse of the passage.

Praying always with all prayer and supplication in the Spirit, being watchful to this end with all perseverance and supplication for all saints.

After being introduced to the concept presented by Graham Cooke, I thought of crafting a prayer for my cancer diagnosis when I realized that, indeed, I already had crafted such a prayer.

The year prior to learning about crafted prayers, I prepared a teaching based on the statement my sister Cheryl—who commented that when we find ourselves in the midst of a fiery trial, in an undesirable, perplexing situation—God, our all-wise Father, is endeavoring to do one or combination of the following actions—direct you, inspect you, correct you, protect you, or perfect you. I transformed that statement into a teaching, *A Five-Fold Prayer: Direct Me, Inspect Me, Correct Me, Protect Me, Perfect Me*.

In the message, I discussed each of the five verbs, using scriptures, anecdotes, and personal incidents as well as related music. Each section concluded with a poem, a psalm, expressing my desire toward God concerning that particular verb. I thought of the section, *Protect Me*, as closely related to my present situation. Since the word protect is not found in the King James Version, which I most often use, I thought of using the word deliver instead.

In the Old Testament, the verb deliver means "to pluck out of the hands of an oppressor or enemy; to preserve, recover, remove; to deliver from danger, evil, trouble; to be delivered, to escape." Psalm 31:1-5 is especially encouraging:

> In You, O Lord, I put my trust;
> Let me never be ashamed;
> Deliver me in Your righteousness.
> Bow down Your ear to me,
> Deliver me speedily;
> Be my rock of refuge,

A fortress of defense to save me.
For You *are* my rock and my fortress;
Therefore, for Your name's sake,
Lead me and guide me.
Pull me out of the net which they have secretly laid for me,
For You *are* my strength.
Into Your hand I commit my spirit;
You have redeemed me, O LORD God of truth.

In the New Testament, the word deliver means "to draw or snatch to one's self from danger, to rescue, to deliver." In the poem, *Why Don't Somebody Help Me Praise the Lord?*, I relate that God personally intervened in my life and rescued or delivered me.

With loving arms you reached way down
And snatched me from Satan's outhouse,
Sought me and flat-out rescued me,
Fixed me up in my Father's house.
Why Don't Somebody Help Me Praise the Lord?

In John 17:15, Jesus Christ makes this statement to God, His Father—"I do not pray that You should take them out of the world, but that You should keep them from the evil one."
Matthew 6:13 provides a similar request expressed in what has become known as *The Lord's Prayer*—

And do not lead us not into temptation,
But deliver us from the evil one:
For Yours is the kingdom and the power and the glory forever. Amen.

II Thessalonians 3:3 offers this reminder—

But the Lord is faithful, who shall establish you, and guard you from the evil one.

EMBRACING YOUR LIFE SENTENCE

II Timothy 4:18 makes a similar declaration:

> And the Lord will deliver me from every evil work and preserve me for His heavenly kingdom. To Him be glory forever and ever.
>
> Amen!

This section of the book concludes with an original prayer:

> As a child runs to safety in his father's arms,
> So I, too, run to you, "my shelter from life's storms."
> Lord, I long to dwell with you in the secret place,
> My buckler, my shield, deliverer, my fortress,
> Strong tower, defender, who responds to my prayer.
> For Lord, you are faithful, who will establish me
> And protect me and deliver me from evil.

This particular section of the teaching seemed perfectly crafted to my situation regarding the diagnosis of prostate cancer and the elevated PSA level. I thought of augmenting it, however, when I recalled a passage from II Corinthians 1:9-10 which I added to my arsenal in this area of spiritual warfare—

> Yes, we had the sentence of death in ourselves, that we should not trust in ourselves but in God who raises the dead,
>
> Who delivered us from so great a death, and does deliver us: in whom we trust that He will still deliver us;

I realized the diagnosis of cancer can be seen by some as a death sentence, but the exhortation is not to trust in ourselves but in God who raises the dead, should the death sentence be actually carried out, as it will be one way or another, should the Lord tarry. In actuality, sin is the death sentence which is manifested, not only in cancer but in a whole range of deadly diseases; indeed, the wage of sin is death. Despite this diagnosis, I continued to trust God, that only as He has delivered those who trusted Him in the past and is presently delivering those who continue to trust Him, so will He yet continue to deliver in the future. I rejoiced as I added those verses to the end of the *Protect Me* section of my crafted prayer.

Praying in the Spirit—Power of Perfect Prayer

In the First Epistle to the Corinthians, Paul relates two ways to pray to God: to "pray with the spirit" and to "pray with the understanding." To pray "with the understanding" is to pray in the language one normally speaks, as if you were having a conversation with God. To "pray in the spirit" is to pray in tongues or to pray in an unknown language to you, the speaker, in the tongue of men or of angels, as mentioned in I Corinthians 13:1. Some refer to this spiritual ability as communicating with God in one's prayer language.

I Corinthians 14:15 makes this statement—

> What is *the conclusion* then? I will pray with the spirit, and I will also pray with the understanding. I will sing with the spirit, and I will sing with the understanding.

In this section of I Corinthians 14, Paul continues discussing "spiritual matters" or "gifts of the spirit," referring to speaking in tongues or "giving thanks well." Some have called this perfect prayer or perfect praise.

Paul concludes the Book of Ephesians with a strong exhortation to put on the whole armor of God in Ephesians 6:10-18. For the Christian believer, putting on the whole armor of

God should be applicable to every situation, but this passage had particular application to my specific situation regarding cancer, especially the last verse of the passage:

> Praying always with all prayer and supplication in the Spirit, being watchful to this end with all perseverance and supplication for all saints—

Verse 20 of Jude also makes this reference to praying in the Holy Spirit or the Holy Ghost—

> But you, beloved, building up on your most holy faith, praying in the Holy Spirit.

In Paul's epistle to the Romans, he speaks of praying in the spirit, which bypasses the mind, as a means of expressing that which you cannot adequately communicate in words.

Romans 8:26-28—

> [26] And the Holy Spirit helps us in our weakness. For example, we don't know what God wants us to pray for. But the Holy Spirit prays for us with groanings that cannot be expressed in words. [27] And the Father who knows all hearts knows what the Spirit is saying, for the Spirit pleads for us believers[a] in harmony with God's own will. [28] And we know that God causes everything to work together[b] for the good of those who love God and are called according to his purpose for them.

Throughout this period of time following my cancer diagnosis, there were times I could not clearly articulate a prayer with my understanding, and so I relied heavily on praying in the spirit in addition to praying with my understanding. Verse 28 goes on to explain that as we pray in the Spirit and submit to His guidance, "we know that all things work together for the good, to those who are the called according to God's purpose." This verse has been especially meaningful to me, and I have designated it as my life verse, a verse that anchors my faith and serves as a touchstone to illuminate, assure, uplift, and energize my faith.

Romans 8:28, my favorite verse in the Bible, offers a reminder that because God is good, "we know that all things work together for the good, to them that love God, to them that are the called according to His purpose." So, no matter how bad any situation may appear to be, we know it will work together for our good. My entire ordeal with prostate cancer prayer has been a life-sustaining force as I have endeavored to remain prayerful in all circumstances.

As We Pray

We give thanks to God, the Father of our Lord Jesus Christ, as we pray always for you.
—Colossians 1:3

During these dark times, we focus on the Kingdom,
Established and grounded on a sure foundation.
As we diligently pursue Godly wisdom,
New paths of this Apostolic Reformation
Unfold as the sun rises on the horizon.
Even in turbulent times, we must stay the course.
Aware of consequences of each decision,
We look to God our Father, bountiful resource.
As we renew our minds, we are transformed and change:
With a "kingdom mindset" we now see with new eyes.
Beyond past narrow limits our view is long-range.
We number our days with each sunset and sunrise,
As the Word commands: pray without ceasing, night and day,
Knowing that God always fulfills his will, as we pray.

5

THE FEAR FACTOR: "DO NOT FEAR; I WILL HELP YOU"

Do not fear, for I am with you,
do not be afraid, for I am your God;
I will strengthen you, I will help you,
I will uphold you with my victorious right hand.
For I, the LORD YOUR GOD, WILL HOLD YOUR RIGHT HAND,
saying to you, 'Fear not, I will help you.'

–Isaiah 41:10, 13 (RSV)

Chapter 3, with its emphasis on the soul—the mind, will, and emotions—speaks of dangerous or toxic emotions. These negative mental forces must continually be dealt with, but in my situation with prostate cancer, I was forced to face head on one in particular throughout the healing process: fear. A cancer diagnosis itself evokes great fear because the term cancer too often generates one of the fundamental human fears—the fear of death.

We recognize fear as a common and natural emotional response to potential danger, but if not properly addressed, it can become a deadly emotion with serious consequences. Excessive fear can become crippling and negatively impact our daily lives. I recognized firsthand that unbridled fear is a toxic emotion that limits and inhibits. Pastor Rick Warren describes fear as "a self-imposed prison that will keep you from becoming what God intends for you to be."

Along the path to recovery, I had to confront my fears which seemed overwhelming at times. During this time, I came to a much greater understanding of fear and its potentially negative consequences. Several entries on my blog, *Dr. J's Apothecary Shoppe*, I discuss fear and how the believer should respond to it. Although these entries were written with others in mind, many times I shared the essence of the lessons that God was teaching me.

As with the other factors related to my diagnosis, I first went to the Bible to see what it has to say about fear, and I found numerous reminders that the people of God are to have no fear. The comforting exhortation to "fear not" or "do not fear" occurs 365 times in the Bible, indicating a daily memo from God that we are not to be afraid.

Particularly meaningful to me was a passage from Isaiah 41:10, 13, offering this comforting reminder—

> Do not fear, for I am with you; do not be afraid, for I am your God;
> I will strengthen you, I will help you;
> I will uphold you with my victorious right hand.
>
> For I, the LORD your God, hold your right hand;
> It is I who say to you, "Do not fear, I will help you."

Numerous times when I encountered stressful situations that attempted to cause me to fear, I found encouragement and strength in the Word of God. Psalm 27, my favorite psalm which I committed to memory as a youngster, provided great inspiration and motivation before, during, and after my diagnosis:

Fear and Its Antidote

When we encounter stressful situations that cause us to respond with fear, we are encouraged to seek the strength to overcome any obstacle that attempts to block the path to success. Again, the Psalmist offers this reminder in Psalm 34:5—

> I sought the LORD, and he answered me; he delivered me from all my fears.

Some people, particularly those with challenging health issues, are overly concerned about the future, which can lead to anxiety. We are exhorted not to too concerned about the future or anything, for that matter. Philippians 4:6-7 was another passage I committed to memory and recited to myself over and over when I sensed the need.

Philippians 4:6-7 (NLT)—

> ⁶ Don't worry about anything; instead, pray about everything. Tell God what you need, and thank him for all he has done. ⁷ Then you will experience God's peace, which exceeds anything we can understand. His peace will guard your hearts and minds as you live in Christ Jesus.

As with each of the toxic emotions of life, learn to counteract their harmful effects with the proper remedy. In terms of responding to fear in light of moving in the opposite spirit, we find that love is the perfect antidote. The love of God or *agape* is the highest form of love, "a love which is more intimate than friend, or kin or wife;" This close-knit love is known as *agape,* a term used exclusively in the New Testament, to reveal the uniqueness of God's love.

With love, as with any other emotion, there must be a demonstration or manifestation whereby one knows the reality of the emotion in question. We speak of the love of God in manifestation which is so clearly demonstrated in one of the most widely recognized verses in the Bible, John 3:16:

> For God so loved the world that He gave His only begotten son, that whosoever believes in Him should not perish but have everlasting life.

It has been said that you can give without loving, but you cannot love without giving. Indeed, all love *is* giving. The essence of love as defined by giving is also seen in this poem by John Oxenham—

> Love ever lives, outlives, forgives,
> And while it stands with open hands it lives.
> For this is love's prerogative:
> To give and give and give

The book of I John also reveals the perfect connection between fear and love, particularly in 1 John 2:5 (NKJV).

> But whoever keeps His word, in him truly the love of God is perfected in him. By this know that we are in Him.

In those who hear the Word of God and keep it, the love of God is perfected or made perfect or complete, wanting in nothing or brought to maturity in them. To be perfected is to be brought to a full end.

The love of God is perfected or made complete or full in us when we walk in the steps of Jesus Christ, the ultimate example of perfect love. Verse 18 provides the basis for love being the perfect antidote to fear.

> There is no fear in love; but perfect love casts out fear, because fear involves torment. But he who fears has not been made perfect in love.

When an individual is perfected in love and walks in or demonstrates that love, there is no room for fear. The love of God is the key that releases each believer from the bondage of this self-imposed prison from which Christ came to set the captives free.

I recall learning about the love of God as a counteractant to fear in an effortless yet profound way. One of the first books my wife and I used to teach our daughters about our Heavenly Father was *My Little Golden Book about God*. This was a kind of primer for our daughters who memorized the words and associated them with the illustrations long before they could actually read. Some of the most cherished lines were these words which closed out the small book—

> Do not fear. I am here. And I love you, my dear. Close your eyes and sleep tight. For tomorrow will be bright. All is well, dear child. Good night.

This simple response encourages all children of God to have no fear, for God is ever present, and He continues to say, "and, I love you, my dear." Even in distressful and disturbing situations where we do not clearly understand what is transpiring in our lives health-wise and otherwise, we must remember there is no fear in love.

THE FEAR FACTOR

There is No Fear in Love

There is no fear in love; but perfect love casts out fear, because fear involves torment. But he who fears has not been made perfect in love.

—I John 4:18

There is no fear in love; but perfect love casts out fear
And abounds to transform any adverse atmosphere.
We are perfected and made whole when we walk in love,
A true love that we live and not one we just speak of.
Such love is pure and never repels but draws us near.

This balm of love heals all wounds, no matter how severe
With words of compassion each soul on earth longs to hear;
Love conquers any disaster and rises above.
There is no fear in love.

We follow in Christ's steps, knowing our mandate is clear.
Assured of triumph, there is never a need to fear.
We press toward the mark, the prize we seek to lay hold of
To ascend in victory on wings of a gentle dove.
We walk forth as bold pioneers on a love frontier:
There is no fear in love

6

THE FAITH FACTOR: WITHOUT FAITH IT IS IMPOSSIBLE

The Christian journey, from start to finish, is a journey of faith.

—Watchman Nee

While working on the subject of fear in Chapter 6, I remembered a quote from years ago by the Methodist missionary, E. Stanley Jones—"fear is sand in the machinery of life." In locating the exact statement, I found extensive comments that believers are designed to have faith and not fear. Rev. Tony Cooke in his message *You are Fashioned for Faith* cites these comments which serve as a springboard to our discussion of faith—the foundation of our belief system—

> I am inwardly fashioned for faith, not for fear. Fear is not my native land; faith is. I am so made that worry and anxiety are sand in the machinery of life; faith is the oil. I live better by faith and confidence than by fear, doubt

and anxiety. In anxiety and worry, my being is gasping for breath–these are not my native air. But in faith and confidence, I breathe freely–these are my native air. A Johns Hopkins University doctor says, 'We do not know why it is that worriers die sooner than the non- worriers, but that is a fact.' But I, who am simple of mind, think I know; we are inwardly constructed in nerve and tissue, brain cell and soul, for faith and not for fear.

Watchman Nee, early 20th Century church leader and teacher in China, describes the life of each believer in this way—"the Christian journey, from start to finish, is a journey of faith." As we journey through life, we encounter challenges designed to build our faith. Believers are on a journey that takes us from faith to faith, glory to glory, and victory to victory as we pursue the will of God for our lives.

Romans 1:17 reminds us of this truth—

> For in it the righteousness of God is revealed from faith to faith; as it is written, "The just shall live by faith."

Throughout my encounter with prostate cancer, I was keenly aware of importance of faith, in that this diagnosis challenged me to go to God and seek His guidance and direction as never before. In reflecting on the unfolding circumstances since that time, I recall being asked to write an article sharing what faith means to me. Here is an excerpt from one of the blog entries based on that original article—

Faith—The Bedrock of My Life

To build a magnificent mansion that will last a lifetime, the builders must begin with a solid foundation. Similarly, to build a purposeful life of success and fulfillment, we must establish a firm foundation upon which we build. For me, faith is the bedrock of life. I define faith as confident assurance, trust, and conviction in God that I will prevail. Faith—"the substance of things hoped for, the evidence of things not seen"— operates beyond what we see, for we walk by faith, not by sight.

Faith is a *Sine qua non*—that without which there is nothing. Faith is the indispensable ingredient in a successful Christian's life. The scriptures remind us that "Without faith it is impossible to please Him. For he that comes to God must believe that He is and that He is a rewarder of those who diligently seek Him."

In the midst of thundering echoes of "No!" faith says "Yes!" Voices shout "You can't!" but faith proclaims "I can and I will!" At the point of total exhaustion, faith says, "Take one more step." After more failed attempts than you can number, faith gives you the courage to try one more time. Faith is tenacious; you hold on and never give up. Although the diagnosis, bank statement or other evidence says, "no way!" faith responds with "God will make a way."

We can find excellent examples of illustrations of faith in the Bible. We begin with Abraham, the father of faith, who did not stagger at the promise of God that he should become the father of many nations, with descendants without number. Despite the circumstances of this hundred-year-old man with a barren wife of comparable age, Abraham grew strong and was empowered by faith. Hebrews 11 recounts the triumphs of men and women of faith in what has become known as the Hall of Faith.

Aside from the Bible, we can glean from the lives of great men and women who achieved impossible dreams. Despite a barrage of reasons why they would fail, they transformed failure into success. Notable examples are the Wright Brothers and countless others, who persevered in faith to accomplish the impossible. We are also surrounded by real heroes who live by faith each day to make a difference.

THE FAITH FACTOR

Without faith it is impossible . . . but with faith, the impossible becomes possible. Indeed, as Christian believers, faith is our solid foundation. Like the wise man who built his house on the rock, when the storms of life approach, if we have laid a firm foundation, the house that we build will stand, for faith is our sure foundation.

Faith: Remember Your Creator in the Days of Your Youth

Whenever I think of faith as a biblical concept, my mind goes back to a Wednesday youth night at Camp Gray, a Presbyterian camp in Saugatuck, MI, when I was a sophomore in high school, back in the day. When the request came forth for a young person to deliver a short inspirational message, I volunteered, and I put together my first Bible teaching on the topic of faith. Using the Bible and study material of one of the camp counselors who was a seminary student, I focused on Hebrews 11:1, 6—two verses that have contributed to the foundation upon which I have built my life as a teacher and minister of the Gospel of Jesus Christ. Since that time 67 years ago, I have discovered the Amplified Bible, and I especially appreciate how these verses are rendered—

Hebrews 11: 1, 6—

> [1]NOW FAITH is the assurance (the confirmation, the title deed) of the things [we] hope for, being the proof of things [we] do not see and the conviction of their reality [faith perceiving as real fact what is not revealed to the senses].
>
> [6]But without faith it is impossible to please and be satisfactory to Him. For whoever would come near to God must [necessarily] believe that God exists and that He is

the rewarder of those who earnestly and diligently seek Him [out].

In 2004, four years after my cancer diagnosis, quite providentially I was asked to teach during a mid-week Bible study at our church at the time when our senior pastor was out of town. He had begun a series on the gifts or manifestations of the spirit from I Corinthians 12, and I was asked to teach on faith.

I opened the teaching by reminiscing with our congregation, as we examined the Word of God and pointed out significant illustrations of faith in the scriptures and in my life. I endeavored to relate the simplicity of faith, being that of hearing from God by way of the written Word or the Bible or by revelation from God. By acting upon what you have heard, you receive the corresponding results of your actions. Romans 10:17 reminds us of the source of faith—"so then faith comes by hearing and hearing by the word of God."

In the early days following my diagnosis, I developed my own 40-day prostate protocol to lower my PSA. During this time, I only happened to come across the tape of that particular teaching and listened to the tape over and over, in an effort to build my faith.

In that teaching, I examined many accounts in the Gospel of Matthew where Jesus Christ mentions faith. Two of the most notable examples occur in the encounter with the centurion who comes to Jesus Christ with a request to heal his servant and the account of the Canaanite woman who seeks Christ's healing presence on behalf of her daughter who is "grievously vexed with a devil." In both these instances, Jesus Christ responds, describing both of them as having "great faith."

Such Great Faith—Crazy Faith

You can also find excellent examples of illustrations of faith in the lives of great men and women who achieved impossible dreams. Despite a barrage of reasons why they would fail, they transformed failure into success. Without faith it is impossible . . . but with faith, the impossible becomes possible. We recognize and rejoice, knowing that with God all things are possible.

Recently, I discovered Richie Parker, a Beauford, SC native, who was born without arms. Not only did this remarkable young man learn to do what some said was impossible—ride a bike—but, he also learned to drive a car. Not only did he drive a car, but he went on to work as an engineer on NASCAR's most award-winning team. Richie commented, "I don't know that there's anything in life that I can't do; it's just a whole lot of things I haven't done it yet." His life is a vibrant illustration of living by faith to accomplish the impossible.

As believers, we sometimes encounter circumstances that seem impossible, and our response is that we know the situation will turn out favorably, despite what appears to be a hopeless case. The world might respond to our positive expectations with, "That's crazy!" We know, however, that we walk by faith and not by sight, and we counter with "That's not crazy. . . That just means we have crazy faith."

Dennis Marquardt states, "Crazy faith is the kind of faith that will respond to God in obedience no matter how crazy it may seem at the moment! It is the kind of faith that CAN remove mountains, and even more amazingly, it can move man!"

When asked what he means by "crazy faith," faith writer Larry King offers this definition—"crazy faith is when you simply refuse to let what you perceive—that is, your circumstances, your situations, your trials, tests, and obstacles—interfere with what you believe."

Bishop Charles Mellette states that walking by faith in such conditions, ". . . doesn't make sense, but it does make great faith." Crazy faith, I might add.

For an illustration of such crazy faith in the Bible, let us look at an individual who is not listed in the Hall of Faith of Hebrews 11. In fact, this person is an altogether unlikely candidate who is described as having great faith. In the context in which the designation was spoken, you might characterize the person as having crazy faith. The centurion in Matthew 8 comes to Jesus Christ with a request to heal the man's servant. In response, the Lord says that he will go and do as he asks. Matthew 8:7-10 (AMP) reveals the exchange between the two of them:

> Jesus said to him, "I will come and heal him." [8] But the centurion replied to Him, "Lord, I am not worthy to have You come under my roof, but only say the word, and my servant will be healed. [9] For I also am a man subject to authority [of a higher rank], with soldiers subject to me; and I say to one, 'Go!' and he goes, and to another, 'Come!' and he comes, and to my slave, 'Do this!' and he does it." [10] When Jesus heard this, He was amazed and said to those who were following Him, "I tell you truthfully, I have not [found such great faith [as this] with anyone in Israel.

With his belief that Jesus Christ only had to speak the word and the results that the officer desired would come to pass, the centurion demonstrated such great faith and profoundly impressed the Lord.

The following poem uses Matthew 8:10 as its introductory verse or epigraph and also makes reference to a question asked by Jesus Christ in Luke 8:8b: ". . . Nevertheless, when the Son of Man comes, will He really find faith on the earth?"

THE FAITH FACTOR

Such Great Faith—Crazy Faith

When Jesus heard it, He marveled, and said to those who followed,
Assuredly, I say to you, I have not found such great faith, not even in Israel!
—Matthew 8:10 (KJV)

As servants of a king assess his vast treasure,
When the Lord returns, will he find faith on the earth?
When He appraises our faith, what will it be worth?
When all is said and done, may we add our measure,
Though small as the grain of a tiny mustard seed.
Should the Lord come during the Age of the Gentiles,
May our faith be found so pure that nothing defiles.
May we be living by faith in word and in deed,
For God is ever faithful and His Word is true.
May such great faith descend from the centurion
To the faithful ones who bear this criterion:
Whatever God shall speak, this shall He also do.
We will still be walking by faith, not by what we see,
While pressing toward the mark, reaching toward our destiny.

PERSONAL PROPHETIC WORDS

Since coming to know the Lord Jesus Christ as my Lord and Savior, I have endeavored to live my life as a man of faith. I recall hearing the term applied to me on a most memorable occasion. In 2000, I received a personal prophecy from Dr. Kingsley Fletcher regarding the dimension of faith in my life. A personal prophecy or prophetic words are inspired words from an individual operating the gift of prophecy to speak to a specific individual or group. These insightfully penetrating words are revealed by God and provide edification, exhortation, and comfort to the individuals to whom they are spoken.

On this specific occasion when Dr. Fletcher ministered at our church, he called me forth and spoke a message from God to me. I transcribed those words and added them to my prayer journal/scrapbook. Numerous times I read and re-read those words as I prayed after being diagnosed with prostate cancer that same year. I especially concentrated on this excerpt—

> The anointing of the Lord is upon you. You shall walk through doors, and you shall bring the people of God behind you. No man shall be able to stand before you all the days of your life. Mighty man of faith! When you declare, it shall be done. You shall affect many through your faith, for out of the faith you shall see my faithfulness. . . . And you shall declare this is the way of the Lord, and they shall follow. For you shall stand and declare just as Caleb declared. You shall stand and say, 'If God said it, it shall come to pass. If God declares it, I believe it. If God points the way, I will follow.' And the people of God shall be inspired by your humble faith. For you are a man that has pleased me, and I'm delighted in you. This is the word of the Lord to you, Lonnell. To Lonnell, the word of the Lord. You shall walk in faith and not by sight.

I used that particular prophetic word as a contact point for focused intercession regarding my specific situation with the prostate cancer, which proved to be a time of the testing of my faith.

At times when my faith seemed to be diminishing, I recited scripture and listened to teaching tapes; in many cases, these were my own messages I taught myself over and over again. During this time of intense prayer, God was teaching me a valuable lesson about faith—prayer is the key, but faith unlocks the door. I was reminded of these lyrics from an old gospel song, as I prayed fervently throughout this situation which seemed to be drawing from within me to become the mighty man of faith God called me to be.

In the same way that fear has been described as "sand in the machinery of life," you could say unbelief is a monkey wrench that could sabotage an individual's destiny. We note what occurred to the Children of Israel as they prepared to enter the Promised Land after forty arduous years of wandering in the Sinai Wilderness—only Caleb and Joshua were allowed to enter the place they had so long desired to access in their journey from the bondage of Egypt. The remainder of the Israelites died in the Wilderness, at the edge of the Promised Land.

Faith in God, believing His promises, and acting upon them gets God's attention. On the other hand, when we fail to demonstrate our faith, our confidence, our trust in God, and His word, our actions displease God. The Book of Hebrews also provides striking examples displaying the devastating consequences of falling into unbelief—"so we see that they were not able to enter [into His rest—the promised land] because of unbelief *and* an unwillingness to trust in God." Believers today are warned to take heed, brethren, lest there be in any of you an evil heart of unbelief, in departing from the living God.

The Gospels illustrate the corrosive and destructive effect of unbelief. This pervasive negative attitude caught the attention of Jesus Christ and caused him to marvel at those in his hometown of Nazareth and the surrounding areas where he was because of their unbelief.

In another instance, after the Lord Jesus Christ had been raised from the dead, he appeared to the eleven disciples later and reprimanded them, calling them to give account for their unbelief and hardness of heart.

Romans 4:20—in the Amplified Bible—speaks about unbelief in light the faith of Abraham, the Father of Faith—

> He staggered not at the promise of God through unbelief;
> but was strong in faith, giving glory to God;

Charles Finney, Professor of Theology and President of Oberlin College from 1851-1865, described unbelief as sin, a voluntary state of mind that he contrasts with faith which "respects the promises of God, it is a confident assurance that they will be fulfilled.... Unbelief is the opposite of this. It is a withholding of confidence from what God says; it is distrust; it is a refusal to commit or give up the mind to the influence of a truth or promise."

Unbelief has been said to be "the only thing that defeats the promises of God." This statement reminds me of a passage from 2 Corinthians 1:19-20 (New Living Translation)—

> 19 For Jesus Christ, the Son of God, does not waver between "Yes" and "No." He is the one whom Silas, Timothy, and I preached to you, and as God's ultimate "Yes," he always does what he says.
>
> 20 For all of God's promises have been fulfilled in Christ with a resounding "Yes!" And through Christ, our "Amen" (which means "Yes") ascends to God for his glory.

One of the most powerful words in the English language, in my estimation, is *yes*. Used to express affirmation or assent, yes often indicates an affirmative reply. Certainly, we are aware of it as a strong expression of joy, pleasure, or approval. When a player scores the winning shot in an overtime game, often excited fans respond with a vigorous "Yes! Way to go!"

In faith, we respond to every promise with a resounding "Yes, God can, and yes, God will!" We say "Amen!" to that. The expression used throughout the Bible means "It is so!" On the other hand, unbelief counters with "Maybe He will and maybe He won't—You never know." The difference is clear.

THE FAITH FACTOR

Faith believes and acts on the promises of God expecting to receive all that has been promised. Unbelief, however, hesitates and questions, responding with uncertainty and limited or negative expectations.

Throughout my ongoing health challenge with prostate cancer, I endeavored to read the Word of God and apply it, by committing it to memory and hiding it in my heart. In the same way, I countered negative or toxic emotions by moving in the opposite spirit in a positive direction. During a time when I was keenly aware of the negative forces of unbelief in my life, I was inspired to write this poem—*Unbelief, the Thief*—which helped me understand what was taking place.

Unbelief, the Thief

For what if some did not believe? Will their unbelief make the faithfulness of God without effect?

[4]*Certainly not! Indeed, let God be true but every man a liar. As it is written:*
"That You may be justified in Your words,
And may overcome when You are judged."
                                            —Romans 3:3-4

As a leech would siphon the life force from our blood,
This insidious culprit clings to our belief,
To undermine our confidence that God is good.
This unwelcome foe invades our mind as a thief,
A bold embezzler, defiling our faith with doubt;
This robber goes undetected, misunderstood.
So we search for each negative to wipe it out,
For a little leaven slowly grows and corrupts
The measure of our faith and gradually weakens
Our trust in God's promises and subtly disrupts
Assurance, though faith still increases and strengthens,

EMBRACING YOUR LIFE SENTENCE

As muscles respond to an exhausting workout.
But we will capture and behead this ungodly thief
And undo his "un" to make solid our belief.

In reflecting on my life's journey thus far, I have learned so much about faith. One of the principal lessons is that life is a walk of faith which I express in this closing psalm, *By Faith*.

By Faith

Look at the proud; his soul is not straight or right within him, but the [rigidly] just and the [uncompromisingly] righteous man shall live by his faith and in his faithfulness.
—Habakkuk 2:4 [Amplified Bible]

The practical aspect of faith is a walk, a lifestyle:
Moment by moment, we walk by faith, not by what we see,
Knowing that this kind of faith propels us to victory.
Even though some may misunderstand and seek to revile,
The shield of faith counters fiery darts of the enemy's thrust.
We trust God, despite all the hinderer might do or say.
Being fully persuaded, we learn to trust and obey.
We persist and obey: signs of our perpetual trust,
For faith directly reflects our relationship with the Lord.
Walking from victory to victory will not seem odd,
For whatever we desire according to the Word,
We shall have when we pray and put our trust in the Lord.
For true faith comes by hearing and hearing the Word of God.
God is faithful and always comes through, just as the scriptures saith:
Obey, persist and sacrifice—the just shall live by faith.

7
THE FORGIVENESS FACTOR: A FORGOTTEN COMPONENT

Forgiveness is both a decision and a real change in emotional experience. That change in emotion is related to better mental and physical health.

–Everett L. Washington, Jr

In responding to a life-threating disease such as cancer, forgiveness can be a spiritual component of the healing process that is sometimes overlooked. During the first ten years of dealing with my prostate cancer diagnosis, I was also a writer for an Internet publication that is no longer operational. I would report on current events, local happenings, and my views from a spiritual perspective. I recall publishing a series of articles on forgiveness. It was not until much later, when the publication had folded, that I realized forgiveness can be a contributing factor to the healing process, and that it could have personal application to my medical situation.

One of the articles I wrote focused on National Forgiveness Day and brought out some significant information about forgiveness, a vitally important concept not only in Christianity but one with universal implications as well. Described as a two-way street, the virtue of forgiveness is eloquently expressed in the Lord's Prayer: "Forgive us our trespasses, as we forgive those who trespass against us." This subject is connected to some of the last words that Jesus Christ, who was also brutally slain, as he spoke before his death on the cross: "Father, forgive them, for they know not what they do."

In addition, Paul also exhorts believers to "be kind one to another, tenderhearted, forgiving one another, even as God for Christ's sake has forgiven you." Dr. Arch Hart, Christian psychologist, offers a definition of forgiveness that seems to be particularly applicable—"forgiveness is giving up my right to hurt you for hurting me."

James E. Hurst cites Dr. Sidney Simon who offers this definition of this critical concept—"forgiveness is freeing up and putting to better use the energy once consumed by holding grudges, harboring resentments, and nursing unhealed wounds. It is rediscovering the strengths we always had and relocating our limitless capacity to understand and accept other people and ourselves."

Forgiveness: What it Means and More

Something else occurred related to forgiveness during this time. A staff member at the College where I was teaching was part of a program that offered a spiritual retreat to a group of teenagers living at a residence for youth in the area. The retreat focused on a different topic each year, and the prayer focus for that year was forgiveness. My fellow staff member had asked individuals to support her program by signing up to pray for the weekend initiative at specific times throughout the weekend. It happened that my wife was away that weekend, and I was caught up on my class assignments so that I could devote considerably more time praying for the event. I

THE FORGIVENESS FACTOR

ended up preparing a workbook of sorts that included notes with scriptural references, poetry, lyrics, and other sources which formed the focal points for my times of prayer for the weekend with an emphasis on the theme of forgiveness.

Since the occasion was called Epiphany Weekend, I began my time off by examining the term epiphany, and these are some of my notes—

> An epiphany is a sudden intuitive realization or comprehension of the essence or meaning of something. It "the appearance; miraculous phenomenon"; a revelatory manifestation of a divine being; a sudden manifestation of the essence or meaning of something; a comprehension or perception of reality by means of a sudden intuitive realization.

In looking up the above definition, I came across this sentence which gives an example of how the word is used—"I experienced an epiphany, a spiritual flash that would change the way I viewed myself"—Frank Maier. I commented that epiphanies come at the most unlikely times, in the most *unlikely* manner, and in some of the most unlikely places. After an epiphany, one is enlightened to the point that one comes to know for one's self or one comes to know a new reality in a more profound personal way.

Once you see yourself for yourself, you will never be the same. I prayed for the weekend to be a life-changing experience for each person participating in the Epiphany Weekend. Whether as a young person living at the children's residence and being ministered to, or as a member of the ministry team, or as someone who prayed for the success of the weekend, my prayer was that we all would know the love of Christ which passes all knowledge. One aspect of God's love is forgiveness.

As a result of my efforts to be a blessing, I certainly experienced an epiphany regarding my understanding of forgiveness on a deeper level. Little did I know that my efforts would pay off later when I recognized that forgiveness could be a factor in the healing process I was undergoing with prostate cancer.

What does it Mean to Forgive?

To forgive means to send away, dismiss, set free; to acquit by a verdict; to give no punishment to the guilty person and to view the guilty person as if he is innocent. Another definition means to let loose or set at liberty (a debtor).

Simply put, to forgive is to love, and to love is to forgive. Remember, however, that you can give without loving, but you cannot love without giving. I learned this firsthand in a very graphic way when late one night after getting off from work, I was accosted by a man who demanded that I give him my wallet. As I reluctantly complied, do you think I *loved* giving him my wallet? Nonetheless, I complied with his demand that I give. As I recall, when I went to my car, hurt and humiliated, I prayed and asked God to forgive the man who was in such desperate straits that he resorted to robbery.

Literally, to forgive means to "give for." You give to those who choose not to give to you. This poem by John Oxenham expresses a profound truth about love and giving—

> Love ever lives, outlives forgives,
> And while it stands with open hands it lives,
> For this is love's prerogative:
> To give and give and give.

You could keep adding "and give" to the last line ad infinitum, for such love expresses endless giving.

Jesus Christ, of course, is the quintessential example of forgiveness. As he is dying on the cross, having been brutalized and humiliated beyond any atrocious behavior inflicted upon any mortal, among the last words spoken by the Lord are recorded in Luke 23:34—"Father, forgive them, for they know not what they do."

When we practice forgiving, we apply the principle of giving and receiving.

Luke 6:38 relates this principle—

> Give, and it will be given to you: good measure, pressed down, shaken together, and running over will be put into your bosom. For with the same measure that you use, it will be measured back to you.

When we forgive, we also recall another expression of truth by Jesus who said, "It more blessed to give than to receive." In a situation where one person offers forgiveness, and another receives forgiveness, who is most blessed? I often say, "When you choose to give, you cannot lose, but when you choose not to give you cannot win."

FORGIVENESS: JOSEPH, JESUS CHRIST AND ME

While I was dealing with my diagnosis of prostate cancer, I was one of the teachers for the Children's Ministry at our church. I prepared many lessons related to forgiveness, including PowerPoint presentations and craft ideas for each teaching session.

One of the series was titled *Forgiveness: Joseph, Jesus Christ, and Me*, where I answered the question "what is forgiveness?" and provided two examples of forgiveness from the Bible concluding with a response to "how does forgiveness apply to me?"

The Old Testament account of Joseph's dreams and his brothers' jealous rage and over-reaction when they threw him into a pit and sold him into slavery. After years of separation when the brothers thought him to be dead, through divine

EMBRACING YOUR LIFE SENTENCE

Providence Joseph, as second in command in Egypt, is reunited with his brothers in Genesis 50:16-21—

> So they sent *messengers* to Joseph, saying, "Before your father died he commanded, saying, [17]'Thus you shall say to Joseph: "I beg you, please forgive the trespass of your brothers and their sin; for they did evil to you."' Now, please, forgive the trespass of the servants of the God of your father."
>
> And Joseph wept when they spoke to him. [18]Then his brothers also went and fell down before his face, and they said, "Behold, we *are* your servants." [19]Joseph said to them, "Do not be afraid, for *am* I in the place of God? [20]But as for you, you meant evil against me; *but* God meant it for good, in order to bring it about as *it is* this day, to save many people alive. [21]Now therefore, do not be afraid; I will provide for you and your little ones." And he comforted them and spoke kindly to them.

Regarding Jesus Christ, we find an excellent example of forgiveness. As he was dying on the cross, these are among his last words spoken:

Luke 23:34

> "Father, forgive them, for they know not what they do."

In sharing the personal application to the children, I shared that forgiving is applying the principle of giving and receiving.

Luke 6:38—

> Give, and it will be given to you: good measure, pressed down, shaken together, and running over will be put into

THE FORGIVENESS FACTOR

your bosom. For with the same measure that you use, it will be measured back to you.

Another scripture I shared was Matthew 6:14-15—

For if you forgive men their trespasses, your heavenly Father will also forgive you. But if you do not forgive men their trespasses, neither will your Father forgive your trespasses.

Finally, Ephesians 4:32—

And be kind to one another, tenderhearted, forgiving one another, even as God in Christ forgave you.

We also taught the children this song, *Forgiven*—

Forgiven, forgiven, God in Christ Jesus has forgiven me.
Forgiven, forgiven, He loosed my shackles and set me free.
Now that I've been forgiven, what's the least that I can do?
I can be like Jesus, who said,
"Father, forgive them for they know what they do."
Forgiven, forgiven, yes, I've been forgiven.
I've been forgiven, and I choose to forgive.
I've been forgiven, and I choose to forgive.

The lesson concluded with a forgiveness puzzle to reinforce the message.

When you add it all up . . .

No sin is 2 **BIG**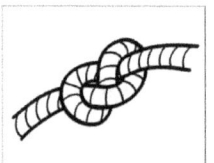

+ 2

———————————————

4 Given

THE FORGIVENESS FACTOR

BENEFITS OF FORGIVENESS

Dr. Robert D. Enright, the founder of the International Forgiveness Institute and pioneer researcher with the first scientifically proven forgiveness program in the country, has developed *Forgiveness Is a Choice: A Step-by-Step Process for Resolving Anger and Restoring Hope*. This study guide demonstrates how forgiveness, when approached correctly, benefits the forgiver far more than the forgiven, indicating that forgiveness can reduce anxiety and depression while increasing self-esteem and hopefulness toward one's future.

The research of Dr. Frederic Luskin, Director of the Stanford Forgiveness Projects, and others has confirmed the benefits of forgiveness in the promotion of psychological, relationship, and physical health. According to learningtoforgive.com, forgiveness has been shown to reduce anger, hurt, depression, stress, and leads to greater feelings of optimism, hope, compassion, and self-confidence. Luskin, the award-winning author of *Learning to Forgive*, introduces techniques individuals can learn "to release unwanted hurts and grudges and open themselves to happiness, peace and love."

Angela Lowe, licensed Christ-centered counselor and consultant in the Central Ohio region, describes forgiveness as a "sacrificial process, not a single one-time, one-way act." In discussing some of the benefits related to forgiveness, Lowe notes that forgiveness enhances the ability to receive and accelerate deliverance, restoration, and healing. She also spoke of numerous physical, emotional/mental, or spiritual conditions, ranging from depression, anxiety, and stress-related disorders to a variety of physical conditions connected to heart and kidney disorders, intestinal problems, various immune disorders, and a list of other chronic conditions impacted by forgiveness.

Forgiving.org also examines *Forgiveness Among Individuals: The Relationship Between Forgiveness and Health* in a series of research projects that study the effects of forgiveness on stress, happiness, coping with major illness, and other aspects of health. Karen O'Connor also discusses the *Healing Power of Forgiveness*. Also, A Campaign for Forgiveness Research acts as a resource for scientific studies related to forgiveness. Everett L. Washington, Jr., Campaign Director, pinpoints the far-reaching effects of this often neglected virtue—

> Forgiveness is both a decision and a real change in emotional experience. That change in emotion is related to better mental and physical health.

Forgiveness of Sins and Healing

In the Bible, there is a connection between forgiveness of sins and healing in the account where Jesus Christ heals the paralytic man who is lowered through the roof to be in the presence of the Lord when the place where he was meeting was grossly overcrowded. The four men who brought this unnamed individual to the meeting devised their bold plan of entering through the roof, and they immediately caught the Lord's attention in Luke 5:20-25—

> When He saw their faith, He said to him, "Man, your sins are forgiven you."
>
> [21]And the scribes and the Pharisees began to reason, saying, "Who is this who speaks blasphemies? Who can forgive sins but God alone?"
>
> [22]But when Jesus perceived their thoughts, He answered and said to them, "Why are you reasoning in your hearts? [23]Which is easier, to say, 'Your sins are forgiven you,' or to say, 'Rise up and walk'? [24]But that you may know that the Son of Man has power on earth to forgive sins"—He said to the man who was paralyzed, "I say to you, arise, take up your bed, and go to your house."

²⁵Immediately he rose up before them, took up what he had been lying on, and departed to his own house, glorifying God. ²⁶And they were all amazed, and they glorified God and were filled with fear, saying, "We have seen strange things today!"

Jesus Christ as the Son of the Living God was sent to into the world for a specific reason—"for this purpose was the Son of God manifest, that he might destroy the works of the devil."

God did not send His son into the world to condemn the world but that the world might be saved from the ravages of sin. As the Savior of the world, he offers salvation, the source of wholeness for the fallen world suffering because of sin. As a result of the fall, a barrage of debilitating diseases plague humanity. All disease ultimately leads to death. On the other hand, Christ, who conquered every sin and all disease—even death itself—offers victory, healing, and deliverance through forgiveness of sin, which he declares to the man in this account.

Another reference to forgiveness of sins and healing is found in the powerful prayer of faith expressed in James 5:13-16—

> ¹³ Are any of you suffering hardships? You should pray. Are any of you happy? You should sing praises. ¹⁴ Are any of you sick? You should call for the elders of the church to come and pray over you, anointing you with oil in the name of the Lord. ¹⁵ Such a prayer offered in faith will heal the sick, and the Lord will make you well. And if you have committed any sins, you will be forgiven.
>
> ¹⁶ Confess your sins to each other and pray for each other so that you may be healed. The earnest prayer of a righteous person has great power and produces wonderful results.

EMBRACING YOUR LIFE SENTENCE

In chapter 4, I speak of the power of prayer, and in Chapter 5, I discuss faith as a critical component in a believer's life. This next passage speaks of the power of the prayer of faith. When two believers prayer requests are in agreement, those petitions are answered, as Jesus Christ declared in Matthew 18:19—

> Again I say unto you, That if two of you shall agree on earth as touching anything that they shall ask, it shall be done for them of my Father which is in heaven.

There is great power in agreement. It goes beyond merely making the same request verbally, but those who are praying are first of all standing together in righteousness, being in right standing with God, and with one another. This passage concludes by recognizing that those whom God has declared righteous offer prayers of great power that produce wonderful results.

OPEN CONFESSION IS GOOD FOR THE SOUL AND MORE

In response to the Scottish proverb "Open confession is good for the soul," Jeffrey E. Miller indicates ". . . it is not merely therapeutic; it is God's prerequisite for forgiveness." The Psalmist illustrates the sinful nature of all humanity and God's willingness to forgive in Psalm 32:5—

Psalm 32:5:

> I acknowledged my sin to you, and my iniquity I have not hidden. I said, 'I will confess my transgressions to the Lord,' and you forgave the iniquity of my sin.

Miller identifies the bridge between our sin and God's forgiveness as "confession." We also note the same connection expressed in 1 John 1:9:

> If we confess our sins, he is faithful and just and will forgive us our sins and purify us from all unrighteousness.

The context for 1 John chapter 1 is fellowship with God and with fellow believers, involving communion or oneness, harmony. In Acts the believers of the early Church were said to be "of one heart and one mind." Having this close fellowship with God and with one another is God's desire for His people expressed in verses 6-10 beginning with the conditional clause "if we" followed by a verb: "If we say…, if we walk…, if we say…, if we confess…, if we say…." These expressions establish the conditions which if met on our part, will result in a corresponding action on God's part. These two parts of the conditional sentences are especially noted in 1 John 1:9. If we do our part, which is confess our sins, our faithful and just God will do His part, which is "to cleanse us from all unrighteousness."

What does it mean to confess our sins to him? The phrase is also translated … "to confess our trespasses … our offenses … our sins." To confess is to say with one's mouth. With our mouths we acknowledge our shortcomings, our misdeeds, our sins of omission and sins of commission. We acknowledge that in far too many instances we have missed the mark and fallen short.

God's ultimate desire is for His creation to stand before Him in righteousness, in right standing before Him without any sense of sin, guilt, or condemnation. Correspondingly, within the human heart is a deep yearning to "get it right," to be all right with God and with one another. Confessing with our mouths our sins to God and to one another positions us to be where God wants us to be and where we want to be.

In thinking about "confession" as a bridge between our unrighteousness and the righteousness of God, one particular confession also comes to mind.

Romans 10:9-10

> [9] If you openly declare that Jesus is Lord and believe in your heart that God raised him from the dead, you will be saved. [10] For it is by believing in your heart that you are made right with God, and it is by openly declaring your faith that you are saved.

This open, honest confession from the heart is not only good for the soul, but a person's whole spirit and soul and body are eternally transformed by that confession.

TOTAL FORGIVENESS:

In his book *Total Forgiveness,* R. T. Kendall states,

> "Forgiveness is not *total* forgiveness until we bless our enemies—and pray for them to be blessed. Forgiving them is a major step; *totally* forgiving them has fully been achieved when we set God free to bless them. But in this, we are the first to be blessed, and those who totally forgive are blessed the most."

Kendall first published *Total Forgiveness,* and he indicated that part of "Total Forgiveness" involves not only forgiving ourselves, but forgiving others, including our enemies, and he went on to say, we must forgive God. Since publishing the initial volume, Kendall has produced a trilogy of books on the topic:

His discussion of "forgiving God" generated considerable controversy. After reading the entire book and re-reading the section on "forgiving God," I understood to a greater degree how this particular focus on forgiving could be a factor when anger, disappointment, and resentment surface when believers encounter what Kendall calls the "betrayal barrier." Such negative emotions may surface in a situation such as a cancer diagnosis or some other potentially devastating disease or in a tragic accident or some other misfortune.

Although I consider myself a deeply committed believer with a passion God, I recognize that certain situations in my life have unfolded in ways that I had expected. After fervently praying, I was perplexed and questioned why my prayers were not answered in the way I thought they would be. In all honesty, I was angry to a degree, and I experienced disappointment for a brief period. Kendall describes such feelings: ". . . our perception is that we are betrayed. In other words, some of us *feel* betrayed. And, as strange as it may sound, we must forgive God if we feel that He has betrayed us."

Chapter 4 of *Embracing Your Life Sentence: Life's Greatest Tragedies into Your Greatest Triumphs* discusses the concept of crafted prayers whereby a person goes to the Bible and finds scriptures that relate to the situation being prayed about and fashioning a personal prayer. During the time following my diagnosis, I crafted this prayer of forgiveness, the most difficult prayer I have ever attempted to articulate.

A Crafted Prayer of Forgiveness: God, I forgive You

God, my Father, gracious God of great loving kindness and the epitome of tender mercy, You forgive each one of all my iniquities, thank you for Your patience. I also praise You for Your understanding the words of this prayer which is so difficult for me to articulate when I say "I forgive You" for all those times in my immaturity and lack of understanding when I questioned You and doubted that You were aware of the deep suffering and humiliation that I was going through. I forgive You for each seemingly inexplicable situation whereby I did not accept and embrace Your love because I did not understand that Your ways are not my ways, when I challenged Your will and questioned that You loved me. Even though I do not fully understand what I am trying to say, I know that You forgive me when I say "I forgive You."

> Though I may have offended unknowingly,
> I give up my right to hurt you because you hurt me.
> As God in Christ Jesus has forgiven me,
> I release all past hurts and I set you free.
>
> I forgive you.
> I forgive you.
> I forgive you
> I forgive you.
> I forgive you this time.
> I forgive you each time.
> I forgive you.

If I have offended You or misspoken in composing this prayer of forgiveness, I know that You read between the lines, as You search me, O God, and know my heart, as You try me and know my thoughts, as You discern with Your Word the depths of my soul and lead me in the paths of righteousness, in the way everlasting, in the name of Jesus Christ, in whom we have every victory, even the final victory.

Reflections on Forgiveness:

In reflecting on my encounter with prostate cancer, I recognize that I have learned invaluable lessons, particular regarding forgiveness and its connection with the healing process. In writing articles and preparing to teach on the topic, I gathered priceless information that I would later apply to my own situation. I also recognized the dual aspects of forgiveness: "To forgive and to be forgiven." Most importantly, I discovered some of the benefits that come to those who practice forgiveness, both in terms of improved mental and physical health. In addition, I examined the connection between forgiveness of sins and healing in the Bible. Finding out about "Total Forgiveness" and its components was also particularly enlightening. One of the most valuable lessons learned is that forgiveness is a choice, as we conclude with this psalm:

I Choose to Forgive

And be kind to one another, tenderhearted,
forgiving one another, even as God in Christ forgave you.
Ephesians 4:32 (NKJV)

I choose to forgive and to release from payment,
To clear the account and forego the debt once more.
Though rightfully owed to me, I choose to forgive,
To be gracious, in spite of the ingratitude.
My desire is to be kind and tenderhearted;
Even as God for Christ's sake has forgiven me,
I rise to the occasion of the Word of God.
Not keeping a record of any wrongs suffered,
I seek to walk in the footsteps of the Savior.
As Joseph, in compassion, assured his brothers
What Satan meant for evil, God fashions for good,
Widen my vision to see a much more grand scope:
May I also see all things working together
For the good, even in perilous times as these.

8

A SETBACK: PERFECTING THE ART OF PATIENCE

"Setback is just a setup for a comeback."

—Walter Jolley

Learn the art of patience. Apply discipline to your thoughts when they become anxious over the outcome of a goal. Impatience breeds anxiety, fear, discouragement and failure. Patience creates confidence, decisiveness, and a rational outlook, which eventually leads to success.

—Brian Adams

A SETBACK: AN "OPPORTUNITY" TO GROW IN MY FAITH

I recall comments made to a student who was facing health challenges because of her back. Unfortunately she had to temporarily withdraw from classes, and I shared this familiar statement: "A setback is just a setup for a comeback." I added, "In any case, God's got your back, and your front, your top and your bottom, and both sides. God's got this!

A SETBACK

God's got you covered." Weeks later, when confronted with an unexpected challenge related to my ongoing battle with prostate cancer, the words of exhortation I shared came back to mind.

On the way to receiving the fulfilment of a promise, we may encounter a problem, an especially challenging situation that takes us by surprise. A number of years ago we were encouraged to view such situations as "opportunities" rather than "problems." I also recall being told that in Chinese calligraphy the characters for "crisis" and "opportunity" are the same. Two individuals confronted with a similar situation may view it differently and label it differently in light of their individual attitude toward the circumstances they face. Standing before me and staring me in the face was an "opportunity" to grow in my faith and overcome yet another obstacle, one more situation where I could be more than a conqueror.

The particular "problem/opportunity" I faced was gross hematuria, or excessive blood in my urine, resulting in a number of trips to the Emergency Room and ultimately being hospitalized. Exactly one week prior, I was honored to share the Word of God at a small church in the area where I teach. As I reflect back on the events that unfolded during that week, I recognize the magnitude of the physical, emotional, and spiritual challenges I faced. Now I see that the entire service was not only an opportunity to share the Word of God, but everything was custom-crafted to prepare me for the grueling week that began that very Sunday.

The teaching centered on Thanks*living*: Universal Antidote for Toxic Emotions ("Stinkin' Thinkin'"). I discuss this concept in chapter 3 of this book related to the truth that "the greatest battles are within." Prior to my teaching the congregation, I experienced a powerful time of worship, as the worship leader introduced the lyrics to "Way Maker," a song offering a series of comparisons declaring who God is and what He will do:

As I lay in the hospital bed, the lyrics resonated within me, touching the depths of my soul as I needed God to reveal Himself and demonstrate these attributes in a very concrete way:

> Way maker
> Miracle worker
> Promise keeper
> Light in the darkness
> My God
> That is who you are

> Lying in the bed, I thought of various scriptures that refer to God's amazing power and might and willingness to come to my rescue.

Way Maker

Isaiah 43:16, 18-19 provide this portrait:

> Thus says the Lord, who makes a way in the sea
> And a path through the mighty waters,
> [18] "Do not remember the former things,
> Nor consider the things of old.
> [19] Behold, I will do a new thing,
> now it shall spring forth;
> Shall you not know it?
> I will even make a road in the wilderness
> *And* rivers in the desert.

Miracle Worker

God, our Father, confirms the gospel of salvation by signs, and wonders and various miracles carried out by Jesus Christ, the Apostles, and by believers who operate the gifts of the Holy Spirit today.

A SETBACK

PROMISE KEEPER

God Almighty, creator of the heavens and the Earth, is faithful and true, the original "Promise Keeper" who cannot lie. The Word of God declares God has given us exceeding great and precious promises that shall all be fulfilled:
   For all the promises of God in Him *are* Yes, and in Him Amen, to the glory of God through us.

LIGHT IN THE DARKNESS

Job speaks this reminder of who God is:
   He reveals mysteries from the darkness and brings the deepest darkness into the light.
   While the Psalmist also declares:
   You, Lord, keep my lamp burning; my God turns my darkness into light.
   The Prophet Isaiah makes known these truths:
   The people who walked in darkness have seen a great light; those who dwelt in the land of the shadow of death, upon them a light has shined.
   I will lead the blind by a way they did not know; I will guide them on paths they have not known. I will turn darkness to light in front of them and rough places into level ground. This is what I will do for them, and I will not forsake them.
   Reflecting on the lyrics to this powerful song of worship inspired this response:

THAT IS WHO YOU ARE.

Way Maker

> Who by His own power makes a way out of no way,
> Out of darkness into the light of a brand new day.
> That is who He is, and that is all we have to say.

Miracle Worker

> Our source and resource of miracles without measure
> From the riches of the glory of His vast treasure.
> To work on our behalf is always His good pleasure.

Promise Keeper

> His will is to fulfill every promise He has spoken.
> We know no word of the Lord can ever be broken.
> Each promise fulfilled is but a foretaste, a token.

Light in the darkness

> We who once sat in darkness have now seen a great light.
> With the light of His Word we put ten thousands to flight,
> Pressing toward a new day when there shall be no more night.

That is who you are

> We long to know you more closely and not from afar.
> We love You and worship You for who you are.

Before the end of the week when I was released, I recognized in a new and even more intimate way that God, my gracious Heavenly Father had made a way out of no-way, and He had once again kept His promise and had shone the light of His Word on my path that led to my release from the hospital once again.

GOD SEARCHES

Throughout the period of time when I was hospitalized, I was blessed to be able to continue to maintain the presence

A SETBACK

of mind and mental stamina to write and post entries on my blog, Dr. J's Apothecary Shoppe and to work on my book. Many times I would post an entry inspired by the Verse of the Day from BibleGate.com or some other source, and the Word shared would minister to me in a most meaningful way.

I recall posting a previous blog entry that focused on the "Word of the Day" which turned out to be "research," whose root is "search", a term related to what God continually does to the human heart. Research, in its most literal sense, means to "re-search" or to "search again. God, our Father, as the ultimate "Researcher" conducts this grand "research project" whose primary purpose is for the advancement of human knowledge about God, that we might "fear God and keep His commandments, for this is the whole duty of man." In the process we discover, interpret, and develop knowledge, which we apply as we grow in our understanding of the Creator and His vast universe. I recall this poem that centers on "searching" or "trying," as in examining closely and scrutinizing in detail in order to render some kind of assessment or evaluation. Introducing the work is a section of Scripture from Romans 8:27-28 (NKJV):

> 27 Now He who searches the hearts knows what the mind of the Spirit is, because He makes intercession for the saints according to the will of God.
>
> 28 And we know that all things work together for good to those who love God, to those who are the called according to His purpose

God Searches

Romans 8:27-28
God searches the depths of each soul and probes each heart,
To uncover each motive and extract the pure,

EMBRACING YOUR LIFE SENTENCE

Discarding dross, thus perfecting the refiner's art.
The word of prophecy stands as even more sure,
The touchstone to measure the essence of all life.
All else shall fail, but the Word shall ever inspire.
This two-edged sword, sharper than a finely honed knife–
Living, powerful, piercing each thought and desire,
Penetrating soul and spirit, joints and marrow–
Probing deepest emotions, dispelling the dark.
Life-giving and powerful, swift as an arrow
That finds its target and that always hits its mark
Reaching its own perfection, to its fullest extent,
The Word of God prospers wherever it is sent.

In thinking about God as "the ultimate researcher," Psalm 139 also comes to mind. The Psalmist opens with recognizing that God knows all about us. Verses 13-16 reveal the intricate and delicate complexity of His matchless creation:

> You made all the delicate, inner parts of my body
> and knit me together in my mother's womb.
> Thank you for making me so wonderfully complex!
> You watched me as I was being formed in utter seclusion,
> as I was woven together in the dark of the womb.
> You saw me before I was born.
> Every day of my life was recorded in your book.
> Every moment was laid out
> before a single day had passed.
> Your workmanship is marvelous—how well I know it.

In some Hebrew texts, the reference to the "inward parts" or "inmost being" in verse 13 has been literally translated "kidneys", the seat of inner human desires. Indeed, we are "fearfully and wonderfully made."

Most amazingly, during this time I was also a patient undergoing a cystoscopy, an example of a deep internal examination

A SETBACK

of parts of the urinary tract. This surgical procedure allows the urologist to examine the lining of the bladder and the urethra by means of a device equipped with a camera and a light inserted into the urethra. Such advances in medical technology make possible the deep probing of our "inward parts" in the natural.

Spiritually speaking, all of Psalm 139 can be viewed as an invitation to deepest, divine inspection, as the celebrated psalm closes with this heartfelt request:

Psalm 139:23-24 (NLT} :

> 23 Search me, O God, and know my heart;
> test me and know my anxious thoughts.
> 24 Point out anything in me that offends you,
> and lead me along the path of everlasting life.

This passage, in part, also inspired this original psalm, an expression of my innermost heart's desire during this very trying time:

Search Me: A Song for You

> *"I know your image of me is what I hope to be*
> *If I've treated you unkindly, can't you see?*
> *That there's no one more important to me.*
> *Oh, won't you please look through me. . ."*
> *"A Song for You"–Leon Russell*

> *Search me, O God, and know my heart:*
> *Try me, and know my thoughts:*
> *And see if there be any wicked way in me,*
> *And lead me in the way everlasting.*
> *Psalm 139: 23-24*

The whole of my life unfolds as an open book,
Known and read by all with eyes to see, page by page.
As you read each line, take an even closer look,
Probe the depths of each of my thoughts, as you engage
The text, searching my heart for its deepest meaning.
Your searching and knowing is the ultimate scan.
As you discern my essence, my inmost being,
I will align myself according to your plan.
Beyond scans, scopes, devices to diagnose,
You see and assess any abnormality.
In these times of watchful waiting, you draw me close:
Despite what tests reveal, you will heal and deliver me.
At times I'm overwhelmed and don't know what to do,
"But we're alone now, and I'm singing this song to you."

Intersection of two feasts: "Taking it Personally":

During the weeks prior to Resurrection Sunday on April 1, the bleeding had returned and I had once again made arrangements to undergo a relatively new procedure to stop the bleeding, but I was uncertain that I wanted to follow through with it. After much prayerful deliberation, I decided not have the procedure done when the bleeding had stopped days before I had initially been scheduled to do it.

Over the course of the week leading up the celebration of the Resurrection, my wife and I visited our daughter and son-in-law and grandson in Virginia. One of the highlights of the trip was attending services at their church where they served communion. Partaking of the Lord's Supper was particularly significant to me in light of my ongoing health issue and my deep yearning to experience healing.

This year the celebration of Christ's resurrection from the dead occurred during the same time Jews were preparing for the start of Passover, the 8-day festival which began at

A SETBACK

Sundown on April 1 and ended on the evening of April 8. Passover, also known as *Pesach*, commemorates the Jewish exodus from Egypt, as families traditionally gather for a Seder dinner, where they retell the story of the escape from slavery, through the plagues, and to the parting of the Red Sea.

Throughout the Old Testament the reference to the Passover Lamb and other aspects of the *Seder* and other events appear as "foreshadowing" or as "types" that unfold in the life of Jesus Christ, the Messiah. Note this reference in 1 Corinthians 5:7-8 (NLT):

> [7] Get rid of the old "yeast" by removing this wicked person from among you. Then you will be like a fresh batch of dough made without yeast, which is what you really are. Christ, our Passover Lamb, has been sacrificed for us. [8] So let us celebrate the festival, not with the old bread of wickedness and evil, but with the new bread of sincerity and truth.

A similar memorable intersection of sufferings of Christ and his ultimate resurrection and the start of Passover occurred in 1998. At that time as a congregation, our church participated in Holy Communion on Good Friday. Although I had observed and participated in the Lord's Supper countless times since adolescence when I first learned the significance of what that observance really meant, on that particular occasion, I took communion and observed the elements of Christ's sacrifice with new eyes. That experience brought to mind Isaiah 53 and 1 Corinthians 5:7, inspiring the following poem which recognizes and personalizes the sacrifice of Jesus Christ on our behalf:

EMBRACING YOUR LIFE SENTENCE

Taking It Personally

Isaiah 53

*"For indeed Christ, our Passover,
was sacrificed for us."
1 Corinthians 5:7b*

Cursed with a curse, He was hung on a tree.
The suffering servant bartered for a price,
Battered and bruised for our iniquity.
Behold the Lamb, unblemished sacrifice,
Offered once, Jesus Christ, our Passover.
Afflicted, stricken, smitten that God should
Freely pour out His mercy, moreover,
Lay on Him the chastisement of our peace.
From His side flowed water and sinless blood,
A new covenant established that we might cease
From dead works by a new and living way.
God's good pleasure no longer concealed
But memorialized this solemn day.
Man of sorrows, with His stripes we are healed.
By the blood of the Lamb we are made whole,
Quickened, cleansed in spirit, body, and soul.

Verse of the Day: Reminder "I am says I am healed."

All during the time I was with my family in Virginia, I experienced no urinary bleeding, but the bleeding recurred and then cleared after having been admitted to the hospital again. The possibility of doing the procedure was once more on the table, but after consulting with my urologist and others, we decided to explore other options by consulting with urologists and oncologists at the University of North Carolina at Chapel Hill, where I made a consulting appointment. While waiting to hear from UNC, I was strengthened and encouraged by the words of another *Verse of the Day* found in 1 Peter 2:24 in the New Living Translation—

> He personally carried our sins in his body on the cross so that we can be dead to sin and live for what is right. By his wounds you are healed.

The New King James Version renders the verse this way—

> Who Himself bore our sins in His own body on the tree, that we, having died to sins, might live for righteousness—by whose stripes you were healed.

1 Peter 2:24 is actually a variation on Isaiah 53:5 (KJV)—

> he was wounded for our transgressions, he was bruised for our iniquities: the chastisement of our peace was upon him; and with his stripes we are healed.

The *Verse of the Day* also brings to mind the reality of the covenant that God made with the Children of Israel expressed in Exodus 15:26 (KJV)—

> And said, If thou wilt diligently hearken to the voice of the Lord thy God, and wilt do that which is right in his sight, and wilt give ear to his commandments, and keep all his statutes, I will put none of these diseases upon thee, which I have brought upon the Egyptians: for I am the Lord that healeth thee.

This verse was the inspiration behind the classic Don Moen song of worship—

I am the God that Healeth Thee
I am the Lord your healer
I sent my word and healed your disease
I am the Lord your healer

The closing words of the verse inspiring this song include the phrase "I am," bringing to mind a powerful life-changing message heard years ago related to our identity, as revealed in the Word of God. At the end of the message, the minister encouraged the congregation to make a list of qualities or attributes that the Bible declares us to be. I personalized the assignment and composed a list of metaphors which opened with the phrase—

"I am. . ."

I am light, the light of the world, sent forth to shine.
I am salt, the salt of the earth, full of savor.
I am alive in Christ; eternal life is mine.
I am blessed: in the midst of famine is favor.
I am trusting in the Lord; I am not afraid.
I am made whole in Christ; by His stripes I am healed.
I am so fearfully and wonderfully made.
I am redeemed, and by the Spirit I am sealed.
I am a sweet savor, a living sacrifice.
I am ever before Him, always on His mind.
I am clothed in righteousness, bought with a price.
I am His beloved, the one He runs to find.
I am cleansed and made whole by the blood of the Lamb.
I am, by the grace of God, what *I am* says I am.

A SETBACK

A Prayer for Patience

Recently while completing this chapter, I came across this quotation about patience, and it caused me to think, and so I want to share these closing thoughts with you—

> Learn the art of patience. Apply discipline to your thoughts when they become anxious over the outcome of a goal. Impatience breeds anxiety, fear, discouragement and failure. Patience creates confidence, decisiveness, and a rational outlook, which eventually leads to success.
>
> —Brian Adams

Throughout the entire healing process of my illness, I have been perfecting the art of patience that involves learning to wait on the Lord. The closing verses of my favorite psalm come to mind.

Psalm 27:13-14 (NKJV)—

> I would have lost heart, unless I had believed
> that I would see the goodness of the LORD
> in the land of the living.
> 14 Wait on the LORD; be of good courage,
> And He shall strengthen your heart;
> Wait, I say, on the LORD!

In the Bible the word for patience has been translated to mean endurance or perseverance, steadfastly bearing up under and remaining faithful while waiting. Patience or perseverance is a fruit of the spirit that should be evident in our lives, as we wait on the Lord.

When we examine one of the words translated—patience—we see a compound word meaning "to stay, remain, abide," literally abiding under. The verb form means to stay under or behind, remain; figuratively, to undergo, that is bear (trials), have the fortitude, to persevere—abide, endure, take patiently, suffer, tarry behind.

The root idea of the noun is that of remaining under some discipline, subjecting one's self to something which demands the yielding of the will to something against which one naturally would rebel. It means cheerful (or hopeful) endurance, constancy—enduring, patience, patient continuance (waiting). It is a bearing up in a way that honors and glorifies our heavenly Father, not merely to grin and bear it.

James 5:11 provides an excellent example of the word for patience being used as a verb and as a noun in an individual who embodies the character trait of patient endurance. The New Living Translation offers this rendering containing a familiar phrase that encompasses a character trait most often associated with Job—

> We give great honor to those who endure under suffering. For instance, you know about Job, a man of great endurance. You can see how the Lord was kind to him in the end, for the Lord is full of tenderness and mercy.

The Book of Job is a classic example of the principle of first usage and first spiritual principle, which highlights as particularly important the first time that a concept is mentioned in the Bible. E.W. Bullinger and other Bible scholars surmise that the first book written was the Book of Job, believed to have been composed by Moses. Job, whom Chuck Swindoll described as a "man of heroic endurance," was a real person, and his story is one of the first demonstrations of many spiritual principles, one of the first being that God is "full of compassion and tender mercy" and that He rewards those who demonstrate patience. Although it is said that patience is its own reward,

A SETBACK

God also rewards patience, as so clearly demonstrated at the end of the Book of Job. Recall Job 42:10—

> And the LORD turned the captivity of Job, when he prayed for his friends: also the LORD gave Job twice as much as he had before.

After being introduced to Graham Cooke and his book on crafted prayer previously mentioned, I recall reading a statement that he made regarding prayer and patience, part of the introduction to the psalm that closes Chapter 8—

A Prayer for Patience

My suggestion for people in a season of birth or upgrade is to write out a prayer for patience and pray it every day.
—Graham Cooke

For you have need of steadfast patience and endurance, so that you may perform and fully accomplish the will of God, and thus receive and carry away [and enjoy to the full] what is promised.
—Hebrews 10:36 (Amplified Bible)

We look back and pause and then look ahead to see
Clearly who God is and who He has called us to be.
We still journey down the road less traveled by
And pray that patience may serve as our trusted ally.
We must say "No" to the pressures of this life
And say "Yes" to the rest God gives, despite the strife.
As we stay our mind on Him, we abide in peace.
When we praise God, works of the enemy decrease.
May we remain and not fall by the wayside as some
But like Job wait until at last our change shall come.

EMBRACING YOUR LIFE SENTENCE

Patient endurance seems delayed for some reason,
But fruit abounds to those who wait in their season.
We pray that in this time of transition and shift
We will embrace waiting as a wonderful gift.

9

EMBRACING YOUR LIFE SENTENCE—MY STRATEGY IN SUMMARY

The closing chapter of *Embracing Your Life Sentence: How to Turn Life's Greatest Tragedies into Your Greatest Triumphs* provides a review of my personal three-fold strategy. First of all, I learned as a watchman to watch, related to the body, the physical aspects of this devastating disease. Secondly, I also learned as a fighter to fight the good fight of faith. We are in a spiritual battle, and the real battlefield is the mind in this section that reviews the mental, emotional components of the soul. Finally, I recognized the spiritual components of my journey, such as faith and forgiveness. Most importantly, as a prayer warrior, I experienced firsthand the power of prayer. Included in the final chapter is a response to being asked if I wanted to continue watchful waiting as my treatment modality, as I share how I arrived at my decision. The book concludes with a poetic self-portrait, including words of exhortation.

John Eldredge in his best-selling book *Wild at Heart* lists three essential characteristics that every man attempts to experience in his life—"A beauty to rescue," "a battle to fight," and "an adventure to live." The last two came into play with my diagnosis of prostate cancer which I describe as "the fight of my life, the fight for my life." My life's journey has thus far certainly been an adventure to live, a remarkable journey of discovery. As I have developed my three-fold strategy, I see how I emerged victorious as a watchman, fighter, and a prayer warrior.

Watchman—Watch Your Mouth and Other Matters

Following my diagnosis of prostate cancer in 2000, I first looked to God for spiritual guidance as to how I should respond. When confronted with any adverse situation, such as the medical challenge, my first step is to go the Bible to see what it has to say about the matter. Ultimately, I always want to learn how the scriptures apply to me and my attempts to deal with the situation that confronts me, for I recognize that the Word of God is practical and profitable.

As my three-fold holistic strategy unfolded, I recognized the importance of three strong action verbs that undergirded my approach—watch, fight, and pray. The first step of my response to prostate cancer was to watch. Throughout the scriptures, I found references to this verb watch. The Old Testament speaks of the importance of watches and watchmen. One of the primary duties of those who watch (or watchmen) was to sound the alarm of an approaching enemy observed from watch-towers.

Similarly, I found I needed to set watchmen on the walls of my life so I could be aware of when the enemy is coming to attack my body or my mind, or any other area of my life. In response to having received the diagnosis of prostate cancer, I found three entry points or gateways of my personal life that I had to monitor or closely watch—the ear gate, the eye gate, and the mouth gate. The picture of the three wise monkeys came to mind to remind me that I must consciously seek to watch what I hear, watch what I see, and watch what I say.

To sum up what I learned about watching strategically, I came across this statement attributed to Frank Outlaw, founder of Bi-Lo Stores. Each line opens with an exhortation to watch. What we are to observe closely could we arranged as an acrostic that can be rearranged to spell W-A-T-C-H—

Watch your thoughts, they become words;
watch your words, they become actions;
watch your actions, they become habits;
watch your habits, they become character;
watch your character, for it becomes your destiny.

I concluded the chapter *Watch Your Mouth and other Matters* with lines from one of my favorite hymns, *Blessed Assurance*, which captures the essence of this approach I chose: watchful waiting or active surveillance—

Watching and waiting, looking above,
Filled with His goodness, lost in His love.

Fighter: In the Fight of My Life, the Fight for My Life

In addition to addressing some of the physical concerns related to cancer, I also had to examine some of the aspects of the soul—the mind, will, and emotions—as they relate to my diagnosis. Topics discussed include the need for an emotional detox program to overcome toxic emotions, which can negatively impact the body's response to cancer. This chapter also speaks of a battle to fight. Relating the battlefield is the mind, I share some of the intense internal struggles I faced. Another related concept is renewing the mind, an ongoing process that must be understood.

Prayer Warrior: Demonstrating the Power of Prayer

This chapter examines the spiritual dimension, focusing on the power of prayer in looking at references from the Bible where believers are encouraged to pray. Also, I discuss crafted prayer and share an example of a crafted prayer composed during the time of my battle with prostate cancer. I go on to discuss specific references to healing in the Bible and how I incorporated them into my prayers.

The Fear Factor—"Do not fear; I will help you"

Chapter 5 discusses fear as a toxic emotion with deadly consequences. The Bible addresses fear with numerous reminders that believers should fear not or have no fear. Many verses are discussed because the term cancer too often generates one of the fundamental fears of humanity—the fear of death. As with each of the toxic emotions previously discussed, this chapter pinpoints the need to counteract the harmful effects of fear with the perfect antidote—the love of God.

The Faith Factor—Without Faith, it is Impossible

Chapter 6 lays a foundation for my holistic strategy with an extended definition of faith as the bedrock of my life. The chapter also examines Hebrews 11 which opens with the quintessential definition of faith and lists notable examples of men and women of God who lived by faith, including Abraham, the father of faith. Another related topic includes the prayer of faith and its relationship to forgiveness, another factor in healing. The chapter also identifies *Unbelief, the Thief* as a corrosive element that can potentially undermine strong faith. The chapter concludes by discussing great faith or crazy faith.

EMBRACING YOUR LIFE SENTENCE

THE FORGIVENESS FACTOR—A FORGOTTEN COMPONENT

In responding to a life-threating disease such as cancer, forgiveness can be a spiritual component of the healing process that is sometimes overlooked. This chapter discusses both aspects of forgiveness—to forgive and to be forgiven—examining notable examples from the Bible, as well as my personal application of the principles of forgiveness. Also, I examine some of the benefits that come to those who practice forgiveness, both concerning improved mental and physical health.

MY DECISION REVISITED

While not directly dealing with my overall strategy, Chapter 8 deals with a series of challenging situations that occurred earlier this year as I was completing the manuscript for my book. I chose not to view each situation as a crisis, but an opportunity—one more situation where I could grow in my faith and be more than a conqueror. Throughout the entire healing process, I have been perfecting the art of patience which involves learning to wait on the Lord.

As a result of repeated episodes of unexpected blood in the urine and subsequent symptoms that led to being hospitalized, I had to respond to these changes in my condition. Following the recommendation of my urologist and other physicians, I made an appointment to consult with a team of urologists at the University of North Carolina at Chapel Hill who looked over my records, including a most recent bone scan and offered their recommendations concerning the issue of prostate cancer.

After making an appointment for my consultation, I received an invitation to share the testimony of my journey with prostate cancer in a filmed interview at *The Truth about Cancer*. I found out about this amazing organization, which I describe as a lighthouse in the midst of the stormy seas of this disease with possibly deadly consequences. I was following my own personalized approach when I discovered this remarkable resource, offering valuable information regarding the history of cancer and its treatment and prevention. I was particularly impressed with voluminous information on alternative treatment protocols, along with a host of inspiring interviews with individuals who have overcome a wide range of cancers, offering hope for those who, like me, choose to follow the road less traveled by. As I approached my meeting with the consultants at UNC-Chapel Hill, the range of options offered to me turned out to be greatly expanded. The timing was also a blessing because both of my meetings most providentially occurred within three weeks of one another.

In discussing my situation, the physicians at Chapel Hill did not advise entirely removing the prostate as an option. Their recommendation was to consider radiation therapy along with hormone therapy as a possibility. As I recall, the option recommended was one of the original options presented to me when I was first diagnosed with prostate cancer back in 2000. If that treatment was not acceptable at that time, and I have managed to live successfully with the situation in terms of my physical, emotional, and spiritual well-being, why would choosing radiation now be an acceptable option?

Concerning possible approaches offered by *The Truth about Cancer*, I recognized that I had been using many similar recommendations which contributed to my success up to this point. My three-fold holistic strategy which God had inspired me to develop and apply involved many of the same approaches toward diet and nutrition, detoxification, the use of herbs and other plant-based organic resources, and other alternative treatment modalities. My connection reminded me of the full range of alternative treatment options available to cancer patients.

The intersection of these two experiences reminded me of a previous situation when I had to determine whether I would continue to pursue watchful waiting or adopt another strategy to address the prostate cancer. I crafted a statement regarding my decision. Now that I face a similar situation, I have revisited my initial response and made some changes which I would like to share at this time.

As with the decision I made when my diagnosis of prostate cancer was first confirmed, I am once again fervently seeking the Lord for guidance and direction. I recall during that time, I participated in a period of prayer and fasting that corresponded to the treatment protocol that I first used to lower my PSA. This daily prayer and devotional schedule ministered to me a great deal and helped me to make my decision. Currently, I am following a schedule of prayer and intermittent fasting, as I continue to seek God's guidance and direction.

At the time of my initial decision, I checked outside sources and reviewed the literature to assist in making an informed decision. I found information revealing that an increasing percent of men diagnosed with prostate cancer, age 74 or older, die from causes other than the initially diagnosed cancer. Research studies at UCLA Department of Urology found that the 10-year risk of dying from causes other than prostate cancer was 40 percent in men aged 61 to 74, and 71 percent in men 75 or older.

I believed this would be the case for me. I recently turned 76, and I firmly believe I will die with prostate cancer but not from prostate cancer.

At the end of Chapter One—*You've Got Cancer*—I shared that I had initially adopted a position of watchful waiting or active surveillance, whereby I would monitor my health and not employ any of the more invasive procedures, such as surgery or radiation to treat the disease. Coupled with this position is my belief that the return of Christ is imminent, as I am "Watching and waiting, looking above." I recall this possibility was echoed by Dr. Paul Taylor, my mother-in-law's surgeon, who remarked "Maybe Christ will return, and we won't have to worry about cancer anymore," as he prayed for her before surgery for colon cancer more than 25 years ago. One of the underlying tenets of my belief system as a Christian is the hope of Christ's return, which fuels and energizes my faith.

Before coming back to Fayetteville four years ago, I underwent a physical examination, and I was blessed to discover that I am in excellent physical condition. One of the doctors who examined me remarked that I was the healthiest thin person he had ever examined and I continue to be in excellent health. For that, I am grateful to God. I maintain a healthy diet which I have modified in light of my diagnosis, and I have established an exercise regimen. My work as a teacher and writer also keeps me mentally in excellent shape. Furthermore, I do not neglect spiritual matters. Indeed, I continue to watch, fight, and pray as a consecrated lifestyle. All these factors are further reasons why I have chosen not to undergo radiation therapy at this point with possible side effects that would adversely affect my physical well-being.

I recognize there is a definite possibility that the cancer will continue to grow and could spread to other organs. Electing not to have the surgery at this point may appear to increase that possibility. Should that occur, I will deal with cancer, un-affectionately called Old Man Crab, as best I can. Having witnessed my brother-in-law's valiant fight as well as the example of my parents and others, I still respond to the dreaded disease with this poetic reminder—

> So git out my face, old man crab,
>   I got your number, don't you see.
> So git out my face, old man crab,
>   I got your number, don›t you see.
> You may win this li'l biddy battle,
>   But we show-nuff got the final victory.

Earlier in *Embracing Your Life Sentence: How to Turn Life's Greatest Tragedies into Your Greatest Triumphs* I mentioned that the diagnosis of cancer is viewed by some as a death sentence, but the Bible exhorts us not to trust in ourselves but in God who raises the dead. The sentence may be actually carried out, as it will be one way or another, should the Lord tarry, "for it is appointed unto man once to die." In actuality, sin is the death sentence which is manifested, not only in cancer but in a whole range of deadly diseases; indeed, the wages of sin is death. In spite of this sobering reality, 2 Corinthians 1:9-10 reminds us—

> Yes, we had the sentence of death in ourselves, that we should not trust in ourselves but in God who raises the dead,
> Who delivered us from so great a death, and does deliver us: in whom we trust that He will still deliver us;

In Chapter One I also recall the words of Norman Cousins, who said: "don't deny the diagnosis, just defy the verdict that is supposed to accompany it." In the face of my diagnosis of prostate cancer, I am determined to continue to watch, fight, and pray. In this ongoing battle, I recall lines from Dylan Thomas: I will "not go gentle into that good night," but I will "rage, rage, against the dying of the light." As I was completing my book, I recalled a poem by Claude McKay, one of the writers of the Harlem Renaissance. Having taught this literary work in many courses, *If We Must Die*, has become even more meaningful to me, especially at this time.

If We Must Die

If we must die, let it not be like hogs
Hunted and penned in an inglorious spot,
While round us bark the mad and hungry dogs,
Making their mock at our accursed lot.
If we must die, O let us nobly die,
So that our precious blood may not be shed
In vain; then even the monsters we defy
Shall be constrained to honor us though dead!
O kinsmen we must meet the common foe!
Though far outnumbered let us show us brave,
And for their thousand blows deal one deathblow!
What though before us lies the open grave?
Like men we'll face the murderous, cowardly pack,
Pressed to the wall, dying, but fighting back!

As I confront the enemy in this final battle of life, I am strengthened and encouraged from the Word of God, knowing that Jesus Christ, our Lord, always causes us to triumph, and we most assuredly have the final victory. Like the Psalmist, I am assured that whosoever trusts in Him will not be put to shame. Arriving at this decision regarding prostate cancer has been another culminating point along this most arduous journey.

I addressed the original document called *My Decision* to my family and closest friends who knew about the decision I was going to make. I closed my response with this request—continue to pray for me, as I endeavor to stay in the will of God, knowing that if God brought me to it, He will triumphantly bring me through it.

This Lonesome Valley

Jesus walked this lonesome valley.
He had to walk it by Himself;
O, nobody else could walk it for Him,
He had to walk it by Himself.

You have to walk this lonesome valley.
You have to walk it by yourself;
O, nobody else can walk it for you,
You have to walk it by yourself.
—Traditional hymn

Valley places are always places of testing....
It's in the valley places that your character is tested.
—Apostle Eric L. Warren

Though there is no place where God's presence does not dwell,
There is this lonesome valley we all must cross alone.
The Spirit drove Jesus into the wilderness,
And as a pilgrim, I, too, go through this barren land.
Propelled by goodness and mercy as my rearguards,
I am led by the hand of God into a wasteland,
Where I must stand on my own and confront my fears,
As I pass through the valley of the shadow of death,
The dark place where no companion can go with me.
Unsure of all that lies ahead, I hesitate,
But I must follow the Spirit's call into the unknown:
The narrow way--to walk by faith and not by sight.
Though my path may be unclear, this I know for sure:
If God brought me to it, He will bring me through it.

EMBRACING YOUR LIFE SENTENCE

MORE THAN A CONQUEROR

I posted a blog entry on *Dr. J's Apothecary Shoppe* on June 4, 2017, the first Sunday in June, which has been designated as National Cancer Survivors' Day. This observance has been set aside as a celebration of life for those who have survived a diagnosis of cancer. In events conducted in communities all over the nation and across the globe, those who celebrate show the world that life after a cancer diagnosis can be fruitful and rewarding. I trust that publishing this book will also bear witness of that truth.

The post focused on what I call the *Word of the Day*, which in this case was survivor. In its most literal sense, the term means "one who survives." FreeDictionary.com offers this series of definitions of the verb "to survive" as an action verb that has an object to receive its action. In this case, to survive cancer—

- To live longer than; outlive.

- To live, persist, or remain usable through any adverse situation.

- To cope with (a trauma or setback); persevere after.

The verb is derived from Latin—*supervivere*, combining the prefix *super* + *vivere*, to live.

Having been diagnosed with prostate cancer in 2000, I have come to understand what it means to be a cancer survivor on a deeply personal level. I recognize a survivor as one who, after encountering an extremely adverse situation, is revived to not only survive but to thrive. Jesus Christ, the ultimate example of a survivor, endured the cross, despising the shame, and after undergoing unimaginable physical abuse, along with the emotional and psychological trauma of the highest degree, arose triumphantly over death itself. Like Christ, I have been revived not only to survive but to thrive, having been transformed from victim to victor.

The true essence of who I am as a believer in Christ is expressed in Romans 8:37, the verse from which the subtitle of this book is derived—"nay, in all these things we are more than conquerors, through him that loved us."

The Amplified Bible puts it this way—

> Yet in all these things we are more than conquerors *and* gain an overwhelming victory through Him who loved us [so much that He died for us].

The expression more than conquerors is translated in the Greek New Testament from the verb *hupernikao,* a compound word with the prefix *huper*—a form of the same prefix found in survive—meaning over, beyond, above exceed, more than. Today, common expressions of the preposition would say over and above or above and beyond. The stem would be *nikao*, translated "to conquer, prevail, overcome, overpower, prevail." Although translated as such, being more than conquerors or super conquerors, is not who we are, but it is what we do, how we live. We completely and overwhelmingly conqueror in the present tense with continuous action; we prevail mightily every day of our lives.

Each year I reflect with gratitude to God for being alive and being able to cherish another year of life. As is my tradition, I sometimes compose a poem of celebration on my birthday. Most remarkably, Romans 8:37 was the epigraph or introduction for a poem composed on my 74th birthday, expressing my new identity in light of the Word for the Day for Cancer Survivors Day and every day I draw breath.

EMBRACING YOUR LIFE SENTENCE

Embracing Your Life Sentence—
More than a Conqueror

*Yet in all these things we are more than conquerors
and gain an overwhelming victory through Him
who loved us [so much that He died for us].*
—Romans 8:37 (AMP)

Embracing Your Life Sentence, more than a conqueror,
Defying the odds as a brave conquistador.
Despite intense pressure I learn to rest in grace,
More than enough to withstand the daily tests I face,
Not merely to survive but to thrive even more.

A mighty warrior, triumphant super victor
With a cause, prepared not to die but to live for.
At times I fell behind but fought to keep the pace:
Embracing Your Life Sentence, more than a conqueror.

To fulfill all the will of God and then to soar
To heights sublime where I have never been before.
Overcomer, bearing light in the darkest place,
I still fight the good fight, as I finish my race,
Moving forward, seeking to find the next open door:
Embracing Your Life Sentence, more than a conqueror.

ACKNOWLEDGEMENTS

Thanking everyone who contributed to the completion of this book would certainly be impossible. Let me, first of all, begin by giving honor to God, my heavenly Father, who first so loved me that He gave His Son, my Lord and Savior, who by his obedience gave his life, and in turn, gave the Holy Spirit, His precious gift, to empower and to comfort and to keep me for all eternity. In addition, I would like to express my gratitude to some of those individuals who have contributed to my life and with whom I share the success of this endeavor: I thank God for my wonderful wife of forty-five years, Brenda Joyce, my love, the wife of my youth in whom I rejoice. We have been blessed with two lovely daughters: Melissa and her husband, William, and our first grandson, Kingston Edward Simkins, have certainly enriched our lives beyond measure. Angela and her husband, Shajuan Joyner, continue to be remarkable sources of joy and blessing.

I also want to thank some of the men of God whose sharing of the Word of God has impacted my life, particularly regarding the development of this book. Over the course of our almost fifty-year friendship Apostle Eric L. Warren's insightful teachings have inspired and motivated me in countless ways. Likewise, I have come to appreciate the Word of God from Pastor Michael T. Bivens, who reinforced the understanding of my spiritual identity in light of who I am in Christ Jesus. I am also particularly grateful for Bishop Charles Mellette of

Christian Provision Ministries whose teaching series on faith was a catalyst that further ignited my passion for sharing from my spiritual journey of faith.

Since moving back to Fayetteville, NC, I have been especially thankful for the Survivors Ministry at Christian Provision Ministry where I first shared my testimony and received encouragement to tell my story and teach the principles of *Watch, Fight, & Pray*. I have also reconnected with Dr. Kevin Bell, a former student whom I first taught more than 40 years ago, who is now a colleague in teaching online courses for Christian colleges and universities. He has been faithful in his encouragement and prayer support.

As I was completing my story, I thought of past and present cancer survivors, heroic men and women whose lives also touched me deeply. My father, Lonnie Johnson, was diagnosed with myeloma and passed away from congestive heart failure, a side-effect of cancer. My mother, Jessie Marie Johnson, a two-time cancer survivor, passed away after a valiant fight against cervical cancer.

I recall my late brother-in-law, Elliott Thompson, who passed away from liver cancer the year before my diagnosis of prostate cancer. My sharing in Elliott's journey with my sister Cheryl, who helped to prepare me for the course of events that I would experience the following year. Another colon cancer survivor is my mother-in-law, Rosa Lee Williams, who ever reminds us that "God is!" Finally, there are many others, family members, and friends, too numerous to name, all champions in their individual battles with cancer.

Being blessed to have overcome the challenge of prostate cancer, I have much to share from my journey of faith. I desire to be an inspiration to those who have been diagnosed with cancer, their family members, friends, co-workers, and others connected with these individuals.

I recall the words of Ralph Waldo Emerson, who speaks of the influence of the poet in his essay with that same title—"the

ACKNOWLEDGEMENTS

poet has a new thought: he has a whole new experience to unfold; he will tell us how it was with him, and all men will be the richer in his fortune."

Although I relate some of my experiences in poetic form, my overall desire is to strengthen and encourage those facing cancer or similar adverse conditions. I trust *Embracing Your Life Sentence: How to Turn Life's Greatest Tragedies into Your Greatest Triumph* will do that and so much more.

ABOUT THE AUTHOR

With a B.S. in Pharmacy from Purdue University, Lonnell Johnson practiced pharmacy for more than 25 years, working primarily in Indiana, Washington, D.C., and North Carolina. In addition, he has also explored a variety of careers, ranging from hospital pharmacist to editor, publisher, and college professor.

Within the past 20 years, however, he has chosen to teach as his primary vocation, having taught on the collegiate level in Kansas, Indiana, North Carolina, Kentucky, and Ohio. Currently, he serves as adjunct professor at Carolina College of Biblical Studies in Fayetteville, NC, where he recently also served an adjunct professor at Fayetteville State University, having formerly served as Associate Professor from 1985-1994, being selected as "Teacher of the Year" in 1989. In 2005, he retired as Professor of English at Otterbein University in Westerville, OH. In addition, he facilitated courses in written and oral communications at National College, University of Phoenix, Indiana Wesleyan University, and Ohio Christian University.

In 2000 after being diagnosed with prostate cancer, he chose to follow the road less traveled by and selected an alternative approach rather than surgery, radiation, or chemotherapy. After 18 years of watchful waiting or aggressive surveillance, Dr. Johnson continues to maintain excellent health. Despite recent challenges, he continues to thrive. As a result, he has much to share with those who may be have been diagnosed with cancer, their family members, friends, co-workers, and others connected with these individuals. He desires to strengthen and encourage those facing cancer or similar adverse conditions. Having learned to "watch, fight, and pray," he has emerged from the battle with cancer, not just a survivor but more than a conqueror.

www.ingramcontent.com/pod-product-compliance
Lightning Source LLC
LaVergne TN
LVHW011842060526
838200LV00054B/4135